BREAKOUT

Finding significance and purpose in your everyday living

Dr Oge Austin-Chukwu
Leadership and Business Coach
Reach Coaching

Copyright © 2017 Dr Oge Austin-Chukwu

ISBN: 978-0-244-94799-6

All rights reserved, including the right to reproduce this book, or portions thereof in any form. No part of this text may be reproduced, transmitted, downloaded, decompiled, reverse engineered, or stored, in any form or introduced into any information storage and retrieval system, in any form or by any means, whether electronic or mechanical without the express written permission of the author.

Publishnation
www.publishnation.co.uk

For Austin, Shona and Daniel

Contents

Preface

Part One – The Desire

The Seed
Start at the Beginning   2

The Root
Part of a Whole   6

The Fruit
Recognising the Itch   10

Part Two – The Path

Step One
You Were Born for This   15

Step Two
Get Rid of the Clutter   20

Step Three
Look in the Mirror   26

Step Four
What Lies Beneath   32

Step Five
Baby Steps   38

Step Six
Who is in Your Circle?   43

Step Seven
Push Past the Pressure   48

Step Eight
Embracing the Mundane   54

Part Three – The Flow

One
Staying Motivated   60

Two
Failing and Falling   65

Three
Making Adjustments   72

Four
Your Best Self   77

Five
Enjoy the Ride   83

Six
Pass it On   86

Conclusion   90

Notes   91

Resources   92

Preface

There are many motivational books out there; I have read my own fair share of them. Some of them were helpful, and some, not so much. I want to start by saying; strictly speaking, this is not a motivational book. I certainly hope it will motivate you to change your life for the better but that was not my primary aim for writing this book. Instead, I want to offer a road map to people out there like me that desperately want to live a life of significance and fulfilment.

If I'm being honest, at first I wondered what qualified me to write such a book, especially with the myriad of other materials out there that address a similar topic. Finally, I decided that after nearly three decades of working with people both as a Medical Doctor and as a Leadership Coach, there were things I had learned along the way that would certainly be helpful to people. Yes, you may well find similar truths in other books, but it won't be written in quite the same way, or with quite the same style.

I like telling stories. I have found that many people learn more easily and remember more when new information is underpinned by an illustration that resonates with them. So I have given many examples in this book from my own personal life and from my work. It was necessary to change the names of the people I used in the stories in order to protect their identity.

I have thoroughly enjoyed writing this book; I hope you will enjoy reading it. But above all, my hope is that you will be set on a trajectory that will take you further than you ever imagined possible. The degree to which this happens will depend in part on how much you engage with the book and how much you allow it to challenge, inform, and inspire you. If it accomplishes all of that, my job would have been done.

Wishing you every success,
Oge Austin-Chukwu
Reach Coaching

Part One

The Desire

"Everyone that has ever done anything significant first found themselves in the place where the status quo no longer was enough."
TemitOpe Ibrahim

The Seed

Start at the Beginning

I stood on the platform, looking out to the sea of eager faces turned towards me. The fact that they were mostly 10- and 11-year-olds did little to calm my racing heart. At one end of the platform stood the headmistress. I could see her from the corner of my eye, although I tried not to look in her direction. To say that I was scared of her would be a bit of an understatement. She represented everything that I was not — confident, imposing and powerful. There were a few other adults that made up my audience of about three hundred. Each class had two teachers present, and they each stood beside their row of pupils, ready to discipline any disobedient child. A part of me wished they were not so attentive — at least they would not notice how nervous and close to passing out I was. The moment there was complete silence, I knew it was now or never. I opened my mouth and began to speak.

The occasion was the Year Six assembly. Once a week, we had the privilege of having the headmistress attend our assembly. The assembly was always held outdoors because we didn't have an assembly hall big enough to hold everyone. Besides, the sun was always out, so why not? Every week, one child from each form had the opportunity to stand on the platform and recite a piece of news or titbit that would be relevant to the other children. It was a way of developing our public speaking skills more than anything else. Every year group had their own weekly assembly, and although by this time I was ten years old, I had always been too shy to even consider volunteering as a representative of my class — until this morning.

What changed? I am not sure exactly. I had always been very shy. It didn't help that I believed I had a bit of a 'weight' problem — I was a bit chubby by average standards. I started dieting when I was maybe eight years old, and a lot of my childhood was spent dieting and exercising in an attempt to lose weight, so that I could look like my slim siblings and friends. So it was really not surprising that I was content with always being in the background, and not drawing any attention whatsoever to myself. It wasn't that I didn't have anything to say — I was just too self-conscious to let my voice be heard; and a lot of my childhood was lived inside my head. Sad, I know; but true, nonetheless.

Back to what changed on this particular occasion. Like I said earlier, I am not sure. But it would appear that I had become fed up with hiding in the shadows. I think a part of me also wanted to prove to myself that this was something I could do. I knew I wasn't stupid, far from it — I excelled at my school work. And I had watched other less smart children (this was my thinking) learn and recite different pieces of news on that same platform week after week. It wasn't rocket science. If they could do it, so could I.

The piece that I chose to learn by heart was a story of some Wall Street magnates in the 1920s that made lots of money but equally lost as much money because of the choices they made. It was a story that was printed and displayed in a gilt frame in our living room. My father wanted us to remember the lessons in the story — and rightly so. For someone who had not done this before, it was very ambitious of me to choose this piece to recite just because of the sheer volume of the words, names and dates that I had to remember. I could easily have made a fool of myself; and that would certainly have crushed me.

There comes a time in your life when you have to do something that amounts to stepping out of the boat. Sink or swim — you'll never know which way it will go until you take the plunge. More often than not, it is not an attempt to impress anyone as much as it is a deep desire to discover what you are really capable of. That discovery is necessary if you are to ever find meaning in your life or have the confidence to pursue your dreams. Although, I was only ten years old, I needed to make that discovery for myself, at least at a very basic level.

And I did. I delivered a five-minute recital that surprised everyone that morning, not least myself. My class teacher looked at me as I took my place once again in line with my other classmates as though she couldn't quite believe what I had just done.

My heart was still pounding, but boy, did it feel good. I had done what I had set out to do. And I had done it well. The seed was sown. I had proved a valuable point to myself and to others, and at that point, I changed the trajectory of my life. Even now I remember that day as though it was a few years ago, instead of the many decades that in actual fact have gone by. While my life did not change dramatically immediately afterwards, something was unleashed inside me that laid the foundation for the person I have since become.

I am not sure why it took me so long to take a step that I felt at the time was a very bold one, and what eventually made me take that leap. Perhaps it was the frustration from years of not using my voice — I don't mean I didn't have ordinary conversations with people — that eventually led to the unusual bravado that I exhibited. Sometimes, you have to get to the end of yourself in order to find your true self. For some, it takes years to get to this place of 'fed-upness'; and for others, decades.

It doesn't really matter at what point in your life you reach this stage. The important thing is that you do get to this point of self-discovery and you do something about it. There is an old proverb that says something like this: *"whenever you wake up, that is your morning."* This is another way of saying that rather than dwell on how long you have been asleep and therefore how much time you might have lost, you instead celebrate the fact that you are finally awake and ready to really live. I guess it is another way of saying, *"better late than never."*

More often than not, stepping out of the boat is not an attempt to impress anyone as much as it is a deep desire to discover what you are really capable of.

Ask yourself:

1. Can I remember a time in my years of growing up when I did something that was out of character?
2. What did I discover about myself through that action or actions?
3. What change did it bring?
4. Re-live the moment and re-learn the lessons.

The Root

Part of a Whole

Just after my GCSE exams, I took a year out because I did not manage to get a high enough score in the university entrance exams to study my degree of choice at the university of my choice. For me, it had always been a career in Medicine, or nothing. Fortunately, I did not have to look very far to find something that would occupy me that year — apart, of course, from studying again for the entrance exams. My mother owned a nursery school, and so I got a temporary paid job there as a nursery assistant.

My role, amongst other things, was to watch over the 3-year-olds while they played outdoors during their break time. Although, this was many, many moons ago, I still remember a little girl called Onyi. At just over 2 years, she was one of the youngest children at the nursery. She had tried more than once to join the older children — including her older sister — in playing. However, she was only little and couldn't keep up with them as they dashed around from one play equipment to another.

It broke my heart to see them ignore her attempts to contribute to their conversations and activities. Somehow, she ended up becoming my little shadow, following me everywhere I went, safe in the knowledge that I believed she had value in spite of the fact that she was only two and could just about walk without falling over. I spent a good deal of time with Onyi and grew to love her as though she were my little sister.

More recently, I have been fascinated by a series on television that video records 4- and 5-year-olds as they interact in a nursery specially kitted out for this purpose. In one of the episodes, one of the four-year-old girls was heartbroken because the other children did not want to play with her, or indeed, pay her much attention. It wasn't that they were being deliberately cruel. She was confined to a wheel chair because of cerebral palsy. Their presumption was that because of her physical disabilities, she was not a valuable playmate; therefore, she did not have a voice that was worth listening to.

Or so it seemed. By the end of the hour-long episode, she had managed to make a few friends and had somehow convinced them that she could contribute significantly to their interactions even if she could not walk. It was impressive to watch how she did this, and it warmed my heart to see her tears turn into laughter. These two examples exemplify what research has found — that deep down, we all have a need to belong, to be accepted, to be seen as valuable members of society, and to contribute in some way to our communities. It's the need for significance.

Abraham Maslow was an American Psychologist born in the early 1900s. He was best known for his work surrounding the creation of a hierarchy of human needs, which is a prediction of psychological wellbeing based on the fulfilment of these needs in order of priority. Maslow's needs are:

> Physiological needs – food, water, shelter, and rest.
> Safety needs – protection, law, order, etc.
> Belonging needs – family, affection, and relationships.
> Esteem needs – achievement, status, responsibility, and reputation.
> Self-actualisation – personal growth and fulfilment.

While this went a long way to explaining the motivation behind our behaviour as human beings, it seemed like there was still something missing. This led Anthony Robbins, an American Life Success Coach, to come up with what he described as the six human needs. These needs are psychological needs that motivate us, at a mostly subconscious level, to act in certain ways. When these needs are met, we experience a sense of fulfilment that is lacking when they are not met.

The Six Human Needs are:

> Certainty – the drive to experience comfort and certainty, and to minimise uncertainty.
> Uncertainty – the need for a little variety and uncertainty as opposed to boredom and sameness.
> Significance – this is an attempt to gain some importance in the eyes of others, and it is closely linked to establishing your identity.
> Connection – lies at the heart of the need to love and be loved by others, and the need to develop meaningful relationships.
> Growth – the drive for new knowledge and experiences that lead to mental, emotional, and spiritual growth.
> Contribution – the need to add value to the lives of others and to be part of something bigger than yourself — something that outlives you.

Each of these needs can have both positive and negative ramifications. For example, your need for uncertainty will generally make you seek variety and new experiences so you don't remain stagnant. This is good because it can help your development in many ways. On the other hand, your need for uncertainty can be so great that you indulge in risk-taking behaviour and intentionally look for crises in an attempt to feed this desire. Similarly, the need for certainty can also mean that you like comfort to the extent where you do not take any risks. While stability and security are good things to have, progress will often require you to step out of your comfort zone every once in a while.

It is interesting to note that two of the six human needs — significance and contribution — were at the heart of the two stories I told at the beginning of this chapter, and they are at play even from a very early age.

You are not exempt. There is a deep desire inside you to be someone of value, and to be seen as such by others in your community. That desire is mirrored by most of the human race, albeit in different ways, depending on age, culture, upbringing, and other variables.

And while there can certainly be negative effects when the need for significance drives people to hurt or attempt to put others down so they can feel important, it is mostly a good driving force. It can provide the motivation for you to strive to be better, do better, accomplish something of value, or build something significant. Tearing other people down so that you can lift yourself above them may be one way of gaining significance, but it will certainly affect other needs adversely — like the need for connection. No one wants to be around a bully, or around someone who is constantly pulling others down. Respect must be mutual and it must be earned.

In the fast-paced world we live in, many of us do not take the time to reflect on the driving forces behind our behaviour. At the risk of over thinking, it is still good practice to take a few minutes at the end of every day to reflect on the actions you have taken during the day. Attempting to uncover the motivation behind your actions will improve your understanding of the forces that drive you. It will give you the opportunity to identify patterns of behaviour that point to a deeper root — a root that might need to be dealt with so that you can move forward without hindrance.

Deep down, we all have a need to belong, to be accepted, to be seen as valuable members of society, and to contribute in some way to our communities.

Ask yourself:

1. Which two of the six human needs are determining my actions the most at this point in my life?
2. What major life decisions have I made in the past that I now recognise were perhaps driven by these needs?
3. Would my decision have been different if I had recognised what need was at the centre?

The Fruit

Recognising the Itch

The five-minute presentation that I told you about in the first chapter of this book shot me into fame overnight — well, sort of. In truth, it was a short-lived fame. Still, all of a sudden, the headmistress and the other teachers wanted to know who this smart — I had reeled off names and dates without referring to any notes — and eloquent 10-year-old was. They also wanted to know where she had been hiding all these years.

I revelled in my sudden, albeit brief, fame, content in the knowledge that I had done what I had set out to do. I had proven to myself that I could memorize a difficult piece of information and deliver it confidently. Job done — or, so I thought.

Within weeks, I had reverted to my old self-conscious, shy, couldn't-say-boo-to-a-goose self. Somehow, my 10-year old mind rationalised that I had proven my point, and so it was all right to go back to the status quo; except that I wasn't content with the status quo any longer. Somewhere on the inside, the desire to use my newfound voice had been awakened. And try as I might, I could not shake off that desire. It showed up in different ways — from joining a drama club, to later on organising events in secondary school, writing articles and short stories, up to my decision to train to be a medical doctor. I wanted to contribute significantly to the communities I belonged to; I wanted my life to count for something.

Some years ago, I worked with a client whom I shall call Mary. Mary had just recovered from a serious health challenge and was looking at her options going forward. It was at this point that she decided she could do with some coaching. She owned her own business at the time but was of the opinion that perhaps she had allowed herself become stressed by her work to the detriment of her health.

As we started to look at what the future might be like for her, one thing kept coming up. While she wanted to continue helping her clients by providing the excellent service she had always given them, there was this desire deep inside to affect more people; to contribute more significantly to her industry and use her skills to affect more people. In her own words, she wanted a 'bigger pond', even if she had to temporarily become a small fish amongst many other fish in that big pond — at least it would afford her the opportunity to grow.

Mary is not exactly unique in the way she felt. Part of the reason so many go through a mid-life crisis is that they get to middle age and suddenly realise they haven't got as much time as they previously thought — time to make their lives count before it is too late. It's like realising during half time at a football game that you haven't scored as many goals as you would like to and half the game has already been played. Sometimes, it takes the death of a loved one, a career change, a serious illness, or a financial crisis to make us stop and reflect on how we are living our lives. 'Are we really living our lives to the fullest?' we ask ourselves.

If the answer is not a resounding 'yes', then something is missing. I call this 'the itch'. I believe most people at some point in their lives experience this itch. For some, it happens early on in their life, while for others, it takes a bit longer for them to recognise that the dissatisfaction they are experiencing is really the quest for a life of significance.

The good news is that it is never too late to change the course of your life. That is, of course, as long as you still have breath in you and are not on your deathbed. I know people in their fifties and sixties who have taken up a new career, started a charitable organisation, started a business, or run for political office. These days people are living well into their nineties, so the term 'middle aged' has had to shift somewhat in its meaning.

In his book, Never Too Late To Be Great, Tom Butler-Bowden says this:

Millions are discovering that they can be active and reasonably independent into their nineties, living to see great-grandchildren come along who statistically can see turning 100 as almost a birthright. The Danish researchers (Kaare Christensen et al) who pointed out this probability also noted that increasing life expectancy is not being accompanied by severe disability. We are not only living longer, but also better management of the aging process means we can enjoy, and be relatively independent in the extra years we are given.

It is also never too early to realise that you have only one life to live and there are no repeats. Malala Yousafzai was only seventeen when she was awarded the Nobel Peace Prize. She was even younger when she became an advocate for girls' education, which resulted in an attempt on her life. While Malala may be exceptional in what she achieved at such a young age, there are many other young people who are making positive contributions to societies, and are using their voices and skills to benefit others.

Ultimately, a life of significance is about the value you bring to others. This quote by Jackie Robinson says it so well: *"A life isn't significant except for its impact on other lives."* It is not about fame, power, wealth, or even pre-eminence. It is not about being popular or trying to please everybody all the time. You do not serve yourself by being anything other than who you really are. A life of significance is not dependent on gender, race, means, or even education or the lack of it. I believe that anyone, anywhere in the world has the potential to live a life of significance. I believe we are all called to do that. The sad fact is that not everyone says 'yes' to that call.

Of course, there is also a benefit to us — the sense of fulfilment that comes from knowing that we are contributing to the success and wellbeing of others. This, however, is a by-product and not the main reason for whatever you do in living out your potential — but what a satisfying by-product!

Ultimately, a life of significance is about the value you bring to others. It is not about fame, power, wealth, or even pre-eminence.

Ask yourself:
1. Where in my life do I sense dissatisfaction?
2. What is happening right now that suggests I might have 'the itch'?
3. Am I living the life I always thought I would or could live? If not, what is stopping me?

Part Two
The Path

For every path you choose, there is another you must abandon, usually forever – **Joan D. Vinge**

Step One

You Were Born for This

You were put on this earth to achieve your greatest self, to live out your purpose and to do it courageously – **Steve Maraboli.**

For some people travelling by train, their preference is to sit facing the direction of travel. I must confess, it is mine also. I like to see what's ahead before I get there; and that goes for life in general — as well as train journeys! There is something to be said, however, when travelling the journey of life, for 'looking back in order to look forward'. Many times, this can give you a better perspective than always looking forward. Let me explain.

Often, when we are in the thick of life — studying, building relationships, starting a family, or climbing the career ladder — we get so busy that we may not see the wood for the trees. We take the next step that seems to make sense without stopping to consider how it fits into the overall big picture. The result is lives that are lived in disjointed compartments that do not seem to connect. The first step to living a life that is meaningful and fulfilling is to be clear about what your purpose on earth is. Without this clarity, you might as well be chasing shadows.

I was 37 years old when I delivered my first full sermon in front of an audience of about two hundred and fifty adults. The subject was one that I was very passionate about, so I was keen to get my points across as eloquently as I could. Prior to this, I had given a few speeches in front of audiences ranging from five to fifty on a variety of topics, but I had not done anything of this scale or magnitude. By this time, I had dealt (to some extent) with the shyness and self-consciousness that constantly plagued me every time I stood up in front of a 'crowd'. But it wasn't until this moment that I really felt like 'I was born for this!' It was a moment of revelation for me as passion mixed with adrenaline completely swamped the nervousness I had felt prior to getting up on the platform. Yes, the first five minutes were rough as I felt all the physical symptoms of 'nerves', but after that, I felt on top of the world; I was still buzzing hours afterwards.

When was the last time you had what I call an 'I was born for this moment'? Looking back at my life before that moment — remember the train journey, facing the rear of the train? — I realised that a lot of things that had happened prepared me for this very moment. I loved teaching; in fact, I came from a long line of teachers, and I derived great satisfaction in finding out all I could about something that interested me, and sharing that information with others.

My little stint at public speaking when I was 10 years old had proven to me that even though I was very shy, I still had it in me to speak in front of a large crowd. After all, there isn't much difference between three hundred 10- and 11-year-olds and some two hundred and fifty adults, is there? And so began my journey into the world of public speaking and training, in both secular and non-profit sectors. Little did I know that years later I would find that experience invaluable in my roles as a Leadership and Business Coach and as a public speaker.

The author of *Never Too Late To Be Great*, Tom Butler-Bowden writes:

'Each of us has foundations that we can build on to create something remarkable. At the time our experiences may seem exactly what we don't want, and only later do we come to appreciate them as building blocks. The key is to take the longer view, and continually ask ourselves how we can use our background and experiences to good end.'

I mentioned earlier in Chapter two, the human need for contribution. Until you are living out your purpose and providing value to others, beyond your own needs and desires, you are unlikely to be satisfied with your life. The desire to make a difference in the lives of individuals or communities runs deep in most people. If you believe in God (or any other form of divine being), it is even more important for you to discover and live out the purpose for which you were created. Discovering this purpose is not always easy, though. In truth, many people spend the first two to three decades of their lives dabbling in different things before settling into what they are really destined for. There are many reasons why this lack of clarity is so prevalent, but one of them is that a lot of people just don't know how to go about discerning their purpose for existing.

What are you passionate about? You can often tell what a person's passion is by what they spend their time and money on! The important thing is not what you say your passions are, it's what takes up a significant portion of your life. Some of you may have to do a lot more digging than others because you have allowed life's circumstances to shape you, which makes you live the life you settle for rather than the one you were called to live. The good news is that it is never too late to rediscover that calling or destiny as long as you are willing to do what it takes.

On the flip side, it may be that there is something that really irks you — something that you would give anything to change. Martin Luther King was troubled by the inequalities of racism. So much so that he gave his life (quite literally) to fight those inequalities. The quote: '*If a man has not discovered something that he will die for, he isn't fit to live*' is attributed to him. What you hate or can't stand is often a clue to the very thing that you are called to change. We may not all be like Martin Luther King but we can still contribute to a change that will benefit society.

Here's an exercise that will help you get some clarity about what you might have been called to do with your life.

Find a quiet place where you will be undisturbed for at least half an hour. Make yourself comfortable. Think about 3 memorable occasions in your past that made you feel excited, fulfilled, on top of the world, and like nothing else mattered except what you were involved in at the time. It could be a moment in time or a period of your life that spanned days, weeks, or even months. Re-live that moment or period in your life. Now, write down the answers to the following questions:

- *Where were you?*
- *What were you doing?*
- *Who else was involved?*
- *What impact did you have on them?*

Once you have done this for each of the memorable occasions or periods, try and find the common thread that runs through them. These could be repeated words, a particular group of people that you appear to be drawn to, or it could be a cause that you were fighting for. This will give you an idea about who or what you are called to. The next step is to try and come up with a short phrase that encapsulates the 'who' and the 'what'. For example, if you find that spending time teaching skills to young people with disabilities to enable them achieve independence is something you love doing, then your phrase might be, *'empowering young, disabled people to live independently with confidence'*. Another example could be, *'transforming lives by awakening people to their true potential'*.

If after the above exercise, you are still unsure of your life purpose, or you need to be absolutely sure, there is another exercise that can help. Think about what you would like people to say about you in your eulogy. Or better still, go a step further and write down the speech you would like your next of kin to read at your funeral. What would you most want to be remembered for? I know some of you may think this is morbid, but it really is a good way of finding out what really matters to you.

This is just the beginning of discovering or re-discovering your life purpose. Don't worry if it sounds cheesy or over the top, it's for your eyes only — nobody else needs to see it just yet. You are still in the blueprint stage and you don't have to share this information with anybody until you have the finished product. If you are feeling brave, however, you could ask your close friends or family what they think your passions are. What have they perceived as common themes in your life in the time that they have known you? All the above exercises serve to do one thing — provide clues that will begin to paint a picture of who you really are and the life you were created to live.

Over the next few days or weeks, go back to what you have written. Make changes to your phrase if you need to. Say the phrase you initially came up with a few times and change the words if necessary until you get to the point where saying those words out loud generates a feeling of excitement and trepidation at the same time. Now, write your phrase on a small card (or on your smart phone if you prefer), so that you can carry it about with you and refer to it often. It will take some time to get used to seeing yourself in light of this new discovery. Well done, you are on your way to a life of purpose and significance!

The first step to living a life that is meaningful and fulfilling is to be clear about what your purpose on earth is.

Ask yourself:

1. What have I discovered about the things that really matter to me?
2. Does this surprise me?
3. How am I going to live differently as a result of this new information?

Step Two

Get Rid of the Clutter

Focus is a matter of deciding what things you are not going to do –
John Carmack

As a species, the magpie does not have a great reputation. In fairness to them, they are very intelligent birds, and the only non-mammal species that are able to recognise themselves in a mirror test. But it is their tendency to be chatterboxes and collectors of any and everything for their nests that puts them in bad stead with humans. They are also known to feed on the eggs and chicks of defenceless songbirds. It is not surprising, therefore, that no one would see being likened to a magpie as a compliment. In fact, according to vocabulary.com, if someone calls you a magpie, it could mean that you are either 'an obnoxious, foolish and loquacious talker', or 'someone who collects things that have been discarded by others' — hardly flattering.

Research has shown that there is a limit to the amount of information the human brain can process at any one time. Angelika Dimoka, director of the centre for Neural Decision Making at Temple University, conducted a study that showed that when information overload becomes too much, the pre-frontal cortex shuts down. This is the part of the brain responsible for making decisions, processing complex thoughts, and controlling emotions. It is located at the front of the brain.

With so many distractions and demands surrounding us in this age of technology, the temptation is to try and do as much as possible in as little time as we can. The truth, however, is that clutter in your life — whether it is the physical clutter of a desk hidden under stacks of paper, or the mental clutter of jumbled thoughts — will stop you from focusing on what is really important. I used to think it was great that I had the ability to multitask. Really, I could even send a text to someone with my mobile phone whilst talking to someone else on the landline. I figured neither of the people could see me, so it wasn't exactly rude. Who was I kidding? There was no way I could give either of those two individuals my full attention, and that was the least I owed them. Multitasking may make us feel like we are somehow smarter than other people, but really, we are not as effective when we try to do a lot of things at the same time as when we focus on a single thing at a time.

Athletes are aware that other than talent and training, doing well requires focus. Attention control is a term that refers to an individual's ability to choose what to pay attention to and what to ignore; in other words, it is your ability to concentrate. When athletes talk about 'keeping your eye on the ball', this is what they really mean. Focus. Focus is almost universally recognised as the number one key to performing well in sports, other than skill and hard work.

In spite of what I said earlier about information overload, the human brain is one of the most complex structures of matter in the whole universe. It is more complicated than the largest computer. This human organ is made up of around 50 to 100 billion neurons or nerve cells that are in constant interaction with each other. There are different parts to this human computer. One of these is the Reticular Activating System or Centre (RAS or RAC) located at the base of the skull. It is one of the most important parts of our brain and it has great influence on cognition. The RAS is the part of the brain where your thoughts, your internal feelings, and the outside influences converge. It serves as a filter for the sensory information you perceive daily so that you do not get information overload.

The Reticular Activating System takes instructions from your conscious mind — like "I need to find a new car" — and passes it on to your subconscious mind, so that the latter becomes alert to that request. For instance, have you ever wondered why the moment you decide you would like to buy a new black VW Golf, you suddenly start seeing black VW Golfs everywhere you turn? This is your RAS at work, making you notice all the black VW Golfs that drive past you. They have been there all the time, only now, because you have a desire to own one, your attention is drawn to them like never before. This is what focus, in the absence of clutter, will achieve.

The things that constitute clutter will differ from one person to another, and from one season to the other. The better you are at selecting what to focus on at any given time, the more effective you will be. It may seem at first that you are doing less, but in the end, you will see the benefits of being very selective about what you expend your energies on.

Matt is a smart young business owner who I coached over a period of about six months. Being a highly motivated and capable person with lots of energy, he could juggle lots of things at the same time. It was no surprise that one of the challenges he faced was how to prioritise what areas of his rapidly growing business to focus on, and what to either delegate to someone else or let go of completely. He had to think seriously about what he wanted to accomplish in his business and the legacy he hoped to leave behind. This meant putting on hold some of the things he desperately wanted to do — like sitting for exams that would give him an accreditation that he didn't really need — in order to concentrate on growing a business he could be proud of. It was a tough decision, especially as the accreditation would give him huge status among his peers. However, studying and sitting for these exams would not only have distracted him from his business, but of equal importance, it would have meant less time spent with his young family.

I believe that there are three types of people: hoarders, minimalists, and those that fit somewhere in between. I tend towards the minimalist end, which means I chuck things and moments later wish I hadn't because I suddenly realise I'd got rid of something I could have used. I have been known to go fishing in the bin for something I discarded a few hours before. Others, like a close family member of mine, can hardly bear to get rid of stuff, even things they no longer have need for.

Not surprisingly, there appears to be a correlation between physical and mental clutter. That's what some researchers at Princeton University Neuroscience Institute found a few years ago when they looked at people's performance in an organized versus disorganized environment. The results of the study showed that physical clutter in your surroundings reduces your ability to focus, and often results in reduced performance. They also found increased levels of stress in people who were working in the disorganised environment.

Other studies have shown similar findings and have even gone as far as to suggest that a physically cluttered environment could lead to depression — but that is beyond the scope of this book. If you doubt the validity of the Princeton University study, I challenge you to tackle a storage cupboard or desk that is in disarray and get some order into it. How do you feel afterwards? Apart from a great sense of achievement at the fact that you have finally got a place of chaos into some sort of order, what do you notice about the clarity of your thoughts?

Clutter is not just physical. In this age of information technology, clogged computer files, applications, and emails can have the same detrimental effect as physical clutter and therefore need to be addressed as well. In my experience, the best way to go about getting rid of clutter is to first of all decide what needs to stay. Whether these are projects, people, or processes, what stays has to be what really matters to you. They also have to be things that serve you well. Some things may seem important often from sentiment rather than their usefulness.

You need to be brutal — anything that is not doing you any good, you have to seriously consider letting it go. It can be helpful to apply the Pareto principle and identify the twenty per cent of things you are involved in that contribute to eighty per cent of the results you see.

I am very selective about the people I spend my time with. Time is precious and I recognise that it is a commodity that cannot always be redeemed. If I am not contributing in some way to a person's life or learning from that person, then I limit the amount of time I spend with them. You may not agree with this, but if you want to live your life with purpose, you don't have the time to hang around timewasters or people that suck the life out of you.

There are some projects and causes that I have had to lay down because I knew I couldn't give them my full attention, and therefore could not do them justice. It was painful to have to say no to some things that I really felt drawn to, but in the end, it was the right decision. It meant that I could then focus on the things that really *really* mattered. So I know first-hand how hard this de-cluttering exercise can be; but it is absolutely necessary for purposeful living.

Once you have decided what stays, then everything else needs to go into either of these two categories: 'put on hold until more appropriate time' or 'get rid of this now'. Do this for projects, tasks; and yes, people. With people, you will obviously have to use some tact — you can't just chuck them in the bin like you would with a piece of paper. Get some assertiveness training if necessary, especially if you need help with establishing clear boundaries in your relationships.

Don't stop there, though. If you've ever owned a garden, you must know that weeding is not a one-time exercise but a practice that has to be undertaken regularly in order to avoid an overgrown and unsightly garden. You will have to regularly re-visit the categories I mentioned above and do some 'weeding' as necessary. When the time is right, you can move something from the 'on hold' group to the 'focus on right now' group. People's capacities and abilities vary considerably but my suggestion would be to focus on one or two main areas of your life, or one or two large projects at any given moment. This will ensure a greater likelihood of achieving success without feeling overwhelmed.

One last word before you attempt this exercise — make sure the workspace where you sit to do this is free of clutter so that you can think clearly. Happy de-cluttering!

Attention control is a term that refers to an individual's ability to choose what to pay attention to and what to ignore.

Ask yourself:
1. What are the areas of my life that I need to focus on right now?
2. What or who are the time-wasters?
3. How can I ensure that I am regularly de-cluttering my life?

Step Three

Look in the Mirror

Mirrors have three purposes. To show you who you are. To show you who you were. And to show you who you want to be." — ***Dan Pearce***

I alluded earlier to the fact that when I was young I was somewhat overweight. I spent a lot of those early years on one diet or another in an attempt to lose some weight. I would like to believe my constant dieting was one of the reasons why I did not grow to the height I could have; I deprived myself of nutrients that were necessary to grow. The results? I am the shortest of my four siblings despite not being the youngest. I remember I did not like having my photograph taken because I would not like what I looked like in them. For the same reason, looking in the mirror was not something I was particularly keen on. This went on for a number of years, until thankfully, I realized that it needed to change. So I started to focus on my good points rather than on my flaws. It was at this point that my self-esteem and confidence started to grow.

Have you ever stood in front of a mirror and wished the reflecting image were different? Mirrors are supposed to show you a true reflection of yourself, unless you happen to be in a hall of mirrors where there are different types of mirrors that distort the image that is reflecting in them. What you see in this instance will depend on what mirror you are looking at. While some mirrors will make you look taller and thinner than you really are — I know you may be desperate to believe that particular mirror, but it is futile to do so — others may make you appear shorter and broader. Tempted as you may be to look in a mirror that distorts your image one way or the other, it is not a true reflection of who you are. We all need mirrors that tell us the truth without any exaggeration or diminution.

Looking in the mirror helps you see what your talents and skills are, and this exercise is a pre-requisite for living a purposeful life. Just in case you were wondering, there is a difference between a person's skill and their talent. Skills are acquired or developed by putting in time and effort while talents are God-given abilities that you are born with. Talents can also be described as strengths.

Marcus Buckingham describes 'strength' in this context as: *"An activity that makes you feel strong. It is an activity where the doing of it invigorates you. Before you do it, you find yourself instinctively looking forward to it. While you are doing it, you don't struggle to concentrate, but instead you become so immersed that time speeds up and you lose yourself in the present moment. And after you are finished doing it, you feel authentic, connected to the best parts of who you really are."*

Both talents and skills are important in determining who you are, and subsequently how you can best serve your family or community. Sometimes, your skills and talents are obvious; other times, they are buried beneath years of life's challenges, disappointments, delayed or broken dreams, and unhelpful criticism from others. If your talents are not readily obvious, what you need is re-discovery as opposed to re-invention. Just as peeling an onion gets you to the core, you need to peel off the layers of whatever it is that has stifled your talents or skills so that what's beneath can reveal itself.

The reason why so many psychometric tests exist is because we need help discovering who we really are and what we are capable of. If you owned a sports car but didn't know that it had the ability to go from zero to sixty miles in three to four seconds, you would never drive it the way it was meant to be driven, and therefore, you would not feel the satisfaction of driving fast. What's more, if you happen to be someone who likes to drive fast cars, you would never really enjoy your sports car to the fullest because you are not using it to its full potential. Both skills and talents are important in determining who you are and what you are called to do.

Engaging in activities that best utilize your skills and talents is very fulfilling. Psychologists have described this concept as being in the flow, or the zone. This flow (or zone) is the mental state of operation in which a person performing an activity is fully immersed in it with focus, complete involvement, and enjoyment. Needless to say, an individual is often most effective in this flow.

Sasha is a young, recently qualified doctor who came to me because her supervisor was concerned that she was not making as much progress as she needed in order to complete the final part of her training as a General Practitioner. One of her main issues was the fact that she was lacking in confidence, and this was affecting her in the workplace; so we started to explore what might be at the root of her difficulties. On the surface, Sasha was attractive, smart and well spoken, but on the inside, she was hugely lacking in self-esteem. A failed relationship in the past and several other disappointments had caused her to draw the conclusion that she was 'not enough' — her own words. The mirror that Sasha was looking in was terribly distorted.

As I dug even deeper, Sasha's real passion started to surface. She had a strong desire to use her medical skills in areas of disaster as a volunteer, but she had not taken any action to make this dream a reality because she thought it was too 'out there' and therefore not within her reach. When she started to look in the right mirror and focus on her strengths and her skills, she realized that the only person that was standing in the way of pursuing that dream was herself. As her confidence in herself grew, she found the courage to end a relationship that she had been tolerating in spite of the fact that it had been a very one-sided affair, one in which she was having to do all the giving without getting very much back in return.

With this draining relationship behind her, Sasha then started to look at the extra training that she would need before she could apply for the volunteer positions she desperately wanted. She also began to look at the contacts she had who might be able to help her with other aspects of her career progression. What changed? All Sasha did was to change the mirror she had been looking into and begin to take control of her own life. Mirrors can lie. If you doubt that, visit a hall of mirrors.

In some cases, other people's perspectives might have been the 'mirror' that you judged yourself by. When I was a young girl, an uncle of mine nicknamed me 'Fatty'. The culture at the time did not frown on adults using nicknames that were not very flattering for children, especially if it was all done in good humour. I wasn't laughing. This nickname affected the way I saw myself for a long time, and it was years before I was able to deal with the damage it had done to my self-esteem.

Whether it was a parent, family relative, teacher, or other people in authority, you may have had people speak words over you that have coloured your view of yourself in a negative way. It's time to shake that reflection off and begin to see yourself differently. Now, I am not advocating deluding yourself into thinking that you are something you are not, I am merely suggesting that you make sure the mirror you are looking in is an objective one.

Joyce Meyer, a minister and leader of a large charitable organization, says, *"Over the years I have learned that a confident person doesn't concentrate or focus on their weaknesses — they maximize their strengths"*. That's what you and I must do if we are going to live the life we were created to live and if we are to get to our final destination in one piece.

There are many ways of discovering what your talents and skills are. As mentioned earlier, there are a myriad of affordable personality profile assessments that you can access either online or offline. I personally use the DISC profile assessment with my clients as it is easy to administer, and the report you receive is equally easy to understand. You don't have to use a formal assessment though — you could ask a trusted and honest friend or colleague to write down what they believe your talents and skills are. I would suggest asking more than one person, and then compare the notes, looking out for recurring themes.

So, what happens if you discover that you have a distorted image of yourself? In coaching language, we call this distorted image "limiting beliefs". Limiting beliefs are any assumptions, perspectives or convictions that are holding an individual back from reaching his or her full potential. These beliefs are usually not based on fact. In truth, we all have limiting beliefs to varying degrees. The first step to dealing with limiting beliefs or distorted images of yourself is to identify what they are. You can't get rid of something if you are not aware of its existence.

The next step is to replace these beliefs with more accurate and positive ones. But be warned, this is going to take some time and a lot of effort. These distorted images or limiting beliefs were not formed in one day. In actual fact, you may have lived with them for the better part of your life and they may be deeply cemented in your psyche. It is going to take commitment and consistent action to replace these images. The good news is that it can be done.

The brain is an amazing organ that can be re-wired because it processes new knowledge all the time. This attribute of the human brain is called neuroplasticity. According to medicinenet.com, neuroplasticity refers to the brain's ability to reorganize itself by forming new neural connections throughout life. It allows the nerve cells in the brain to compensate for injury and disease and to adjust their activities in response to new situations or changes in their environment. This means that we can learn throughout our life, as long as the brain is not damaged by disease, drugs or trauma.

You are more likely to succeed if you involve your family and friends in your makeover. Give them permission to call you up short if they hear you talking about your old distorted image rather than the new improved version. Focus on your talents and skills and work to improve your weaker areas as best as you can. Above all, celebrate who you are. You are the only 'you' that exists or will ever exist, so make the most of you!

The first step to dealing with limiting beliefs or distorted images of yourself is to identify what they are. You can't get rid of something if you are not aware of its existence.

Ask yourself:

1. Am I viewing myself through the correct mirror or is my image of myself distorted?
2. Where is my focus — on my strengths or on my weaknesses?
3. How can I celebrate and use my talents and skills on a daily basis?

Step Four

What Lies Beneath

You begin to fly when you let go of self-limiting beliefs and allow your mind and aspirations to rise to greater heights – **Brian Tracy**

In step three, we looked at mirrors and the negative effects that looking in the wrong mirror can have. I feel like this is an important enough area to warrant a further step to deal with what lies beneath the reflection you see when you look in the mirror. In his book, *The Inner Game of Tennis*, T Gallwey made popular the concept that in sports, the game is first won on the inside before the victory is ever seen on the outside. But even before Mr. Gallwey existed, Napoleon Hill had written about this same concept in his book *Think and Grow Rich*. This idea was not original to Napoleon, as it must be noted that he referred to the timeless classic written and published by James Allen in 1902, entitled *As a Man Thinketh*. Going even further back, the one who must be rightfully credited with this concept that has been proven from one generation to another is King Solomon as recorded in the *Book of Proverbs*, one of the books of the Christian Bible.

The concept is simple; before anything can change on the outside, there must be a change on the inside — in our thinking. During a period of discouragement a few years ago, when circumstances appeared to be against me rather than for me, I was reminded about this concept. Something immediately became obvious to me; I realised that the discouragement I felt inside showed up in my whole demeanour; the words that I spoke, the actions that I took, and my general outlook on life. The result was that the despair that I felt inside increased and somehow my circumstances seemed to worsen as they responded to my feelings. Therein began a vicious cycle that I was not even aware of! Clearly, the only way anything was going to change in my circumstances was if I changed my negative, defeatist thoughts to positive and esteem building ones.

Now, before you dismiss this as a psychological babble, read the next few statements. In a study of clinically depressed patients, it was discovered that 12 weeks of cognitive therapy (which involves reframing a person's thought processes) worked better than drugs, as changes were more long lasting than a temporary fix. Patients who had this training in optimism had the ability to effectively handle future setbacks than those that did not. Also, in a retrospective study of 34 healthy Hall of Fame baseball players who played between 1900 and 1950, optimists lived significantly longer. Similarly, other studies have shown that optimistic breast cancer patients had better health outcomes than pessimistic and hopeless patients. Convinced? I hope you are.

The first step in overcoming limiting beliefs is to identify those beliefs. It is no use thinking you don't have any limiting beliefs. We all do. It's just that we are not always aware of those beliefs or the ways in which they are disempowering us. It is not necessarily a case of right or wrong beliefs because limiting beliefs are not generally judged on a moral scale. Your mindset and your ways of thinking (or thought patterns as they are sometimes referred to) either help you or hold you back. Whether you like it or not, your reality becomes enshrined in what you believe. Somehow, you find evidence to support your beliefs, even when that evidence is not one that will stand up in a court of justice!

Limiting beliefs are acquired as we grow and develop and can be dependent on such things as the family in which we grew up, cultural background, educational experience, past failures, or even successes. Sometimes, those beliefs are so ingrained in our thoughts that we cannot actually remember a time when we thought differently or indeed how we came to hold those beliefs. What you believe about yourself and your abilities is very instrumental in deciding whether or not you succeed at a particular thing.

Studies have shown that the people who succeed at tasks that others would consider, at best, improbable, and at worst, impossible are those who believe that they can. How does this work? Well, no one knows for sure, but it seems that when you believe a particular thing is achievable, your brain goes into action and begins to look for ways to make that particular thing become a reality. The opposite is also true and the moment you believe that something is impossible, your nervous system goes into the 'inactive mode' where it doesn't even try to look for ways of making that thing happen.

Ever heard the story of the four-minute mile? For years, people believed that it was impossible for a human being to run a mile in less than four minutes until Roger Banister proved this wrong in 1954. The amazing thing was, however, that within a year, 37 other runners had broken the belief barrier and achieved the same. The year after that, 300 other runners did the same thing. How did that happen? One person proved that it was possible, and in doing so, changed the belief of others, leading to them achieving the same incredible feat.

Even science recognises the power of belief. Ever heard of the placebo effect? Drugs that had absolutely no potency whatsoever had an effect on some people because they believed that the drug would make a difference if they took it, even though it had no active ingredient in it.

What does this mean? You are either empowered by what you believe, or you are limited by your beliefs. Through your beliefs, you can either create or destroy. You can frame your world by what you believe, and since what you believe determines what you say, what you are saying about yourself matters. It is, therefore, paramount that we regularly check our beliefs and make sure they are not limiting our productivity.

As Robert H. Schuller said, "Today's accomplishments were yesterday's impossibilities." We only need to look at where technology was a few years ago and where it is now to see how true this statement is. The bottom line is this, if you want to change areas in your life for the better, a good place to start would be your beliefs. I mentioned Sasha in the last chapter and her belief that 'she was not enough'. Although this belief was one she held in the area of a personal relationship with a significant other, she couldn't help the fact that it began to rear its ugly head in her work and her confidence at work was significantly reduced as a result.

One of the best ways to identify your limiting beliefs is by asking yourself some questions and answering them as honestly as you can. Sometimes, it can be helpful to have someone else ask you these questions. Start by identifying areas in your life where you may be feeling 'stuck' or where you feel you have not achieved the things you would like to. Even if you cannot identify any areas that qualify (it is extremely rare for this to be the case), go through the questions anyway and jot down your answers.

Questions to Identify Limiting Beliefs

- What negative or pessimistic thoughts reoccur in my mind every time I think about this goal or aspect of my life?
- What assumptions have I made towards making this area or goal a success?
- What rules might I have created in my life that could be stopping me from starting or completing this goal? Or from making this change that is required?
- What reoccurring scripts or narrative am I constantly playing over and over again in my mind? These often include the words 'ought to', 'should', 'shouldn't', 'mustn't', 'never' and 'always'.
- What values am I holding on to despite the fact that they haven't served me well so far?
- What cultural ways of thinking am I holding on to that are restraining me in some way?

> What excuses do I give for not achieving what I would like or for not becoming the person I would like to be?
> Do I have black and white thinking or am I comfortable with some grey?

These are by no means exhaustive, but they are a start as you begin to uncover some of the limiting beliefs you might have. Identifying these patterns of thinking is only the first step but an important step because you cannot correct what you are not aware of. Once you have identified them, the next step is to replace these beliefs with new ones. Your new beliefs have to be ones that empower you and move you forward as you pursue the goals that will help you live a purposeful and fulfilling life. Your new beliefs also have to be believable, otherwise, you won't even believe them yourself!

So the next step is to create new beliefs that are believable, based on some evidence that you have, and ultimately make you feel better about yourself. Here again, you may need help from a coach, mentor, or a reliable friend. We don't always see the good in ourselves and often need other people to point out our good qualities. You can also take the limiting beliefs you identified when you completed the exercise above, and turn them into opposite, more positive statements. Example, 'I am rubbish at relationships' could become 'I work hard to ensure my relationships are rewarding and fulfilling'. Even if you are still in the process of making that new belief a reality, the more you remind yourself of it, the more likely you will become what you believe.

Once you have come up with these new beliefs, you have to cement them into your thoughts. This can be done in a number of ways. For example, you can write them out on a notepad and put them in a place you can see them often. Repeating the beliefs out loud to yourself can also be helpful. The more evidence you have to underpin your new beliefs, the quicker and more likely you will be to assimilate them into your pattern of thinking. Remember that you have held your old beliefs for months (or even years) so it is going to take some time and effort to replace them with new beliefs. However, it can be done.

Other activities that can help you deal with your limiting beliefs include listening to uplifting and motivating talks, collecting quotes that are positive and resonate with you, spending time with positive people (optimism is contagious), reading books that encourage you rather than those that discourage you, and trying not to fill your day by listening to bad news laden with doom and gloom (unfortunately a lot of the news in the media qualifies).

What you believe about yourself and your abilities is very instrumental in deciding whether or not you succeed at a particular thing.

Ask yourself:

1. What areas have I identified in my belief are in need of a change so I can move forward?
2. What am I going to do about my discovery?
3. Who will I ask to help me stay accountable to my answer to question No 2?

Step Five

Baby Steps

The journey of a thousand miles begins with one step – **Lao Tzu**

When my son was about ten months old, he started bottom shuffling. At an age when most other babies would have started to crawl, he completely bypassed that phase having discovered that he could get about just as quickly by shuffling on his bottom using both hands as paddles.

Erroneously, I thought this was going to be a short-lived fad, that sooner or later he would figure out that walking was how most other human beings got from one place to the other — I was wrong. His bottom shuffling went on for another ten months and it wasn't until he was twenty months old that he took his first steps. I was one proud and relieved mother as I watched him take the first few of those steps. Wobbly as they were, those steps were a sign that he was making progress and that he was not going to spend the rest of his life on his bottom!

It doesn't matter how small your first step towards a life lived to the fullest may be, it is progress so long as it is taking you in the right direction. A word of caution — before you take that first step, you need to be clear about where you are headed. In his best-selling book, *The 7 Habits of Highly Effective People*, Stephen Covey writes about Habit number two — *Begin with the end in mind*. The basis of this injunction is that in order to reach the destination you desire, you have to start the journey with that destination in mind. Simple, right? Yet, many of us are living our lives hoping we will end up where we want to be instead of actively planning our journey with the destination in mind.

Steven Covey writes, *"To begin with the end in mind means to start with a clear understanding of your destination. It means to know where you are going so that you better understand where you are now and so that the steps you take are always in the right direction. It is incredibly easy to get caught up in an activity trap, in the busy-ness of life, to work harder at climbing the ladder of success only to discover it's leaning against the wrong wall. It is possible to be busy — very busy — without being very effective".*

The reason I had you complete the purpose determining exercise in step one is that before you take the first step to live out that purpose, it would be helpful to be clear about what that purpose is in the first place. This does not mean that you won't make mistakes, falter, or change course along the way, but at the very least you would have a starting blueprint for what you are working towards. Steps one to three have been about gaining clarity; step four is about taking action.

Five years ago, when I decided to leave my position as the senior partner of a small medical practice, I didn't really have a clue about what I was going to do next. One thing was certain though — I could not carry on with life the way it was at the time. My work had become little more than just a job and I was not enjoying it as much as I felt I ought to. This was in part due to the fact that I was not living out my purpose fully and I was tired of making excuses as to why that was the case.

For weeks, I spent time reflecting, praying, and talking things through with my husband, Austin, who also happens to be my best friend and greatest cheerleader. I didn't want to make any move until I knew exactly what my ultimate goal was. I was fortunate to have taken a payout from the practice partnership, so this meant that there was no pressure for me to make a decision quickly or worry about how the bills would be paid. It was during this time, while attending a Bible college course, that someone asked me if I had ever considered coaching as a career.

It was a chance conversation — or so it seemed at the time, but now I believe it was all in the divine plan — but her question struck a chord in my heart. Up until that time, I had been involved in personal development and mentoring to varying degrees, from one to one mentoring to organizing conferences and workshops. These were things I enjoyed doing, but I had never seriously considered making a living out of these activities. I immediately did a little bit of research on coaching, and I found an organization that offered training that suited my circumstances. Less than a year later, I had my diploma in Corporate and Executive Coaching; and thus, Reach Coaching was launched.

It all started with one step. This step involved taking stock of my life, which subsequently led to the decision to leave my medical practice and go after what my heart was really yearning for — the opportunity to help transform people's lives by supporting them as they pursued their dreams.

Now, some of you may think leaving my job when I hadn't figured out what I was going to do with the rest of my life was a very bold step. In truth, that step was the culmination of many small steps taken before. Steps that involved setting aside time to reflect, talking to people whose counsel I trusted, and taking stock of my finances to make sure I could survive after leaving the practice — if only for a few months. I had also considered the worst-case scenario — if all failed, I could always find another job. It would not be the end of the world.

This may be a good time to stop and expand on the life purpose statement you wrote in step one. Now that you know what you would like to spend the rest of your life doing, it's time to craft your mission statement. This is the opportunity to write in more detail, the actions you will take to become the person you need to be and to do the things you need to do in order to fulfil that life purpose. While your purpose statement will be a sentence or phrase, your mission statement can be as long as you want it to be. You can also add or deduct from it as seasons change or as you become clearer about what you want to do. I have included a template in the appendix.

Once you have written out your mission statement, you are ready to go! You now have a clearer picture of what you want to spend the rest of your life doing; you've got rid of the clutter that might have been distracting you, and you've considered what your gifts and talents are. Ask yourself 'what's my first step?' You can have all the clarity in the world about yourself and what you can accomplish, but until you begin to take action, that thing will remain a dream — like the architect who draws up plans for a house but never actually builds that house.

The first step is often the most difficult. This is because it could involve letting go of the familiar in order to embrace the unknown. There is always an element of fear when we don't know exactly how things will turn out. What happens if things don't work out as I hoped they would? What if I fail? These are common questions that arise whenever we are stepping into something new. Guess what? You will never know until you try. What if I am not ready yet? You'll never feel ready, so you might as well just go ahead and take the leap. Calculated risks are necessary if you ever hope to transform your life — or anybody else's for that matter.

I am not advocating that you take the first action that comes to mind without thinking things through. I sit down with my clients and we map out a strategy using the Stepping Stones tool. This tool helps you consider where you are now and where you would like to end up. In between those two points, you fill in the gap with steps that to the best of your knowledge will connect the two. It's a bit like using a map to plan your journey from one place to another. You may not know with certainty if there will be traffic along the way or road diversions, but you plot your journey anyway and make allowances as best as you can for the eventualities that may arise along the way.

It is important to note that your first step does not necessarily have to be a huge one. In fact, it is best if your first step is a simple one that you can take immediately; one that you are almost certain to complete with a good chance of success. This will give you the confidence to take the next step, and as the steps become more difficult, your confidence will increase. Bottom line, your first step really needs to be a win.

When my client Sasha (mentioned earlier) decided that she wanted volunteering in war torn countries to be a part of her work going forward, her first step was to do some research around what training she would need to undertake in order to qualify for the positions she had seen. This led to her accepting a job in a trauma unit where she could gain experience in the type of medical emergencies she could expect while volunteering in a disaster zone.

You can use the Stepping Stones model to plot your journey to your desired destination. As you begin to take the steps you have mapped out, you may find that some steps need to be altered. Remember that this map is merely a guide, not a straitjacket — so, be flexible. I would recommend that before you turn the page to the next chapter, you make sure you have taken at least the first step of your plan, even if that first step is a baby step. What starts as a baby step ultimately leads to a walking toddler, and eventually, an adult with the ability to run.

It doesn't matter how small your first step towards a life lived to the fullest may be, it is progress so long as it is taking you in the right direction.

Ask yourself:

1. What one thing can I do in the next twenty-four or forty-eight hours that will launch me on the path to my final destination?
2. What skills or resources am I likely to need as I live out the life I have been called to live?
3. How can I acquire those skills or resources?
4. Am I clear about what my destination looks like? If not, why not?

Step Six

Who is in Your Circle?

Be around people who have something of value to share with you. Their impact will continue to have a significant influence – **Jim Rohn**

Bill is an incredibly smart young man in his early twenties. Most of primary and secondary school had been a breeze for him. Without trying too hard, he had aced his GCSEs and A levels. Getting accepted into the university of his choice to study Economics had seemed like a walk in the park, especially to his friends who had not managed to make the required grades to get into their degree and university of choice. Looking on from the outside, it seemed unfair that he had got so far ahead in life without having to work very hard.

It was no surprise that after he graduated from university (of course, he obtained a first class), Bill was offered a job at a top financial institution in the city. In actual fact, he had the promise of the job before he graduated because the company felt he showed such promise. His starting salary and benefits were of envious proportions. He was truly on the road to success, and life was very good for him. One thing was missing, though. Bill had got to a point in his life where he actually needed to put some more effort into his work instead of expecting to just sail through. Trouble was, he wasn't ready to grow up.

For all his enviable high intelligence quotient, Bill was not as wise with his choice of friends as one would have hoped. He had three close friends with whom he spent a fair amount of his leisure time. None of them appeared to have much interest in putting in more than the barest minimum of effort into their work or in carving a career path that had meaning or purpose. Living for the present was their mantra and they relished the relative lack of responsibility youth afforded them. You can probably guess the rest of the story.

Before long, Bill was having too many late nights, too many days off work, and more than his fair share of missed deadlines. He was passed over for promotion several times, and as a result began to see himself as a victim of bad luck. It never once occurred to Bill that his friends might have had something to do with his attitude to life and work.

The story I have just told you is fictitious, but I have come across many grades of 'Bills' in my work, and I am sure you have, too. The people they constantly surround themselves with can influence even the strongest character. The human brain is remarkable in the sense that if it is presented with words or concepts enough times, it will begin to accept these words or concepts as true even if they are not. As you can see, this could have either positive or negative consequences. It explains why brainwashing is possible. If you keep company with defeatists — people who constantly moan about the rotten hand that life has dealt them; who refuse to take responsibility for their lives — guess what? Sooner or later, you will begin to think and talk like them.

Our thoughts are played out in our actions. Cognitive behavioural therapists work based on this premise. They aim to get people to see the link between their thoughts, feelings, and behaviour; then find practical ways of changing unhelpful behaviour. If you think you are unable to do a particular thing, you'll probably prove yourself right. On the other hand, if you think you can, or you can at least learn how to do it given the opportunity, then you most probably can.

As relational beings, we live in communities and find fulfilment in relationships with other people with whom we have things in common. This desire to relate is coupled with the desire to belong, and very often, we will adapt our behaviour in order to fit it. The result is, the more we spend time with that person or persons, the more we become like them. Scary, but true.

It doesn't just stop at the company you keep. The books you read, as well as the information you absorb through other forms of media, also influence the way you think and act. Have you ever listened to a particular song for a considerable length of time, then hours later you find yourself humming it under your breath? Many times, you were not even actively memorizing the lyrics, but, yet, you find yourself singing some of the words almost verbatim!

Jill was a lady that I mentored not long ago. She was having some difficulty dealing with the negative script in her head that said she was never going to be good enough. A failed marriage in her past didn't help matters. As devastating as this had been, to make matters worse, her parents had blamed her for the relationship breakdown and had spoken words that added to her feelings of inadequacy. In the end, Jill had made the painful decision to put some distance between her parents and herself because the constant negativity was destroying her.

In spite of the fact that her parents were no longer nearby, their words had left their mark, and Jill had to learn how to rebuild her self-esteem. Part of her strategy was to surround herself with people who were more forgiving of her failures; people who were committed to speaking positive words about her. Thankfully, she was able to rewrite the negative scripts in her head in order to embrace her destiny. The company you keep can make a huge difference to your success or failure in life.

One of the first people I spoke to about my desire to leave my medical practice in order to pursue other dreams was my mother. A part of me felt guilty at the thought that I was throwing away more than twenty years of training, hard work, and money that I had invested in becoming and practicing as a doctor. My parents funded my six years at medical school, and this made sure I graduated without the burden of a huge student loan. Understandably, I didn't want my mother (my dad had passed away at the time) to feel it had all been a waste.

It turned out I had no reason to be worried about her response. I still remember her words to me, words to the effect that all the experience I had gained over the years would not be wasted. Instead, she believed those experiences would go a long way in ensuring that I succeeded in my next venture. She respected my decision and knew that it was not one that I had made lightly. Since that uplifting conversation, she has continued to be one of my greatest cheerleaders as I continue to attempt to live true to my calling and destiny. She has never been reticent about communicating her belief in me, and I am truly blessed to have her in my 'circle'.

Most people have three or four close friends with whom they spend a considerable proportion of their time. These close friends make up their inner circle of friends. Even the most extroverted amongst us only have a small circle of intimate friends. While you may not have the luxury of choosing your family, you can and ought to be very selective about who you allow into your inner circle. By all means, have as many acquaintances as you like, but when it comes to your inner circle — the people that have access to your dreams and aspirations — make sure these are people that bring out the best in you. Make sure they are people who refuse to allow you settle for mediocrity. They also need to be people who are not afraid to be honest with you or hold you accountable to the high standards that you set for yourself. It goes without saying that you should be willing to do the same for them.

The people in your inner circle are the ones you may want to share your blueprint from step four with. Ask for their support as you go along the path that will ultimately lead to your final destination. Give them permission to ask about your progress and to point out when you are allowing circumstances dictate your progress or when you might be making excuses for not doing your best.

An old proverb says this: 'if you want to go fast, go alone, but if you want to go far, go together'. If you are going to live your life the way you were meant to, then you need people around you. Make sure they are the right kind.

A Dominican University study carried out a few years ago looked at how goal achievement is influenced by writing goals, committing to goal-directed actions and being accountable for those actions. The study looked at 149 men and women of varying ages and from different spheres of life. The researchers found that the group with the most success in achieving their goals were those who not only had their goals written down but also sent a progress report regularly to someone who held them accountable for what they had written down. This study provided evidence for the effectiveness of three coaching tools: accountability, commitment, and writing down one's goals. The bottom line, if you want to succeed, make sure there are people in your circle who will help you stay focused.

If you want to go fast, go alone, but if you want to go far, go together – African proverb.

Ask yourself:
1. Who are the people that make up my inner circle?
2. Are they a positive or negative influence?
3. What am I going to do about the people in my life who do not have a positive influence on me?
4. How can I ensure that I have a positive influence on the people around me?

Step Seven

Push Past the Pressure

Success is to be measured not so much by the position that one has reached in life as by the obstacles which he has overcome – **Booker T. Washington**

If there is one thing you are sure to encounter on your journey to whatever destination you have pictured in your future, it is this — setbacks. I prefer to call them detours. While you may think this is just a play on words, seeing these unplanned challenges as detours rather than setbacks somehow makes them easier to navigate.

There are some days that I wake up and wish I could pull the covers back as far as they will go and go back to sleep. On these mornings, I wonder why I am pushing so hard, trying to cut a way through whatever forest I might be ploughing through at the time. The temptation to give up is so real that I can taste it above my morning 'not so fresh' breath. And yes, although I win the battle most of the time, there are times when I just want to roll over and play dead for just a little while. I am human after all — and so are you.

What you and I must not do is stay in that place of despair longer than is absolutely necessary. Because the longer you stay in that pity party hole whose walls are layered with defeat and self-doubt, the more difficult it is to get out unscathed, and the less likely it would be for you to eventually get to live the life you were made for. I have seen this happen more times than I care to think about. Anyone who has ever accomplished anything of significance knows that you have to push past the bad days in order to get to the finish line in one piece.

A very good friend of mine has a disabled son who requires a lot of care. He often gets unwell and is hospitalized for days and sometimes weeks at a time. My friend is a professional and she is very good at what she does. It would be understandable if she decided that life was too difficult for her to try and pursue her own goals and dreams of making a difference in other people's lives. True, there are some dreams she may not be able to go after at full speed because of the limitations with her son, but she doesn't allow herself become a victim of her circumstances.

Each day, she has a choice to make — she can either push through the obstacles in front of her or she can hide under a shroud of 'why me?' and watch her life peter out into nothing. You and I have a similar choice, every single day. It's the small choices we make every day that determine the direction our lives will take. Regardless of what challenges you face, you alone decide whether what you want is worth fighting for or not.

My first year of running my coaching business was very exciting. I love starting new things — building them from scratch and watching them grow. I was privileged to get my first few clients without having to do much marketing. I was doing what I loved — helping people achieve their dreams — and it was very fulfilling. In contrast, my second year was very lean. It didn't seem to matter what I did, I just could not seem to attract any clients, let alone the right kind. Even a dog would have been a welcome client — except that we didn't have any pets I could coach!

That year, there were many days when I wondered if I had done the right thing — leaving a well-established and rather lucrative career as a General Practitioner. I second-guessed nearly every decision I made — the result was that my confidence as a coach began to dwindle. Many times, I found myself close to giving up my dream of working flexibly while helping other people become all that they could be. I had to remind myself that if I didn't do what I felt I was called to do at that period of my life, I would merely be existing and not really living. So I gritted my teeth and kept pushing, determined that I would not give up on this dream without giving it my best shot. My persistence paid off. Five years later, and many more clients later, I am still enjoying the benefits of running my coaching business.

Recent research seems to suggest that many successful entrepreneurs are not necessarily more talented or skilled than their counterparts who are not quite as successful. Instead, what the successful entrepreneur — or writer, actor, musician, politician, teacher — possesses in abundance is a quality called perseverance; some refer to it as grit. Perseverance is the persistence in doing something despite difficulty or delay in achieving success.

Dr Paul Stoltz, CEO of Peak Learning Inc. and author of *GRIT – The New Science of What it Takes to Persevere*, maintains that you cannot 'get to great without grit'. Dr Stolz spent decades studying entrepreneurs in an attempt to discover what qualities were most likely to help them achieve what they set out to achieve. Time and time again he found that a lot of the entrepreneurs he interviewed had experienced tough challenges. However, instead of letting these challenges stop them in their tracks, they harnessed them to achieve extraordinary results in their businesses.

An ancient proverb says: 'If you fall to pieces in a crisis, there wasn't much to you in the first place.'

Trouble has a way of revealing what lies underneath the surface and uncovering skills and strengths you never knew you possessed. You'll never know if you have what it takes to succeed until you have faced challenges and still managed to come out on top. Problems have a way of forging character like nothing else will. People who succeed are generally those who face challenges head on rather than run in the opposite direction.

Having said all this, perseverance just for the sake of persevering is not what I am advocating. A well-known quote attributed to Albert Einstein says: "Insanity: doing the same thing over and over again and expecting different results." While perseverance is a great quality to have, doing the same thing when it hasn't yielded any results over an appropriate length of time serves no purpose.

There is always something to be learned from setbacks, if you take the time to reflect on them. Flexibility must go hand in hand with perseverance. It is flexibility that enables you to change direction when necessary and to consider other ways of achieving the goals you set out to achieve. It is important to keep an open mind, so when one idea has not worked out like you hoped it would, you would be willing to entertain the thought of doing things differently.

When you are driving and you come across a roadblock, you don't grit your teeth and insist on getting past the barricades; you'll only end up damaging your car — not to mention getting in trouble with the law. Throwing up your hands in the air and crying, 'Well, I am never going to get to this conference (or any other event), I'll just sit here and whine' doesn't help either. That's what a child might do. No, instead, you stop the car, pull out your road map or Global Positioning System (GPS) and try to find an alternate route. If your destination is important to you, you'll find a way to get there somehow.

It is always helpful to be prepared to deal with detours so that when they arise you are not completely taken unawares. This preparation involves first, an attitude of your mind. This is the attitude that believes there is always a solution to every problem that might arise, and therefore you will not allow yourself to be overwhelmed. Next, try and put proven strategies in place for dealing with what could happen when life throws you a curve ball. People handle things differently based on their personalities and the resources available to them. Become aware of your method of dealing with challenges and adjust it to the situation as necessary. Deal with stress in an appropriate manner so that you don't end up burnt out.

My practice (once I have blown off some steam and dealt with the emotional turmoil that invariably follows such a setback) is to take a step back from the situation. I spend some time reflecting on what has happened and how to best deal with it. I also make it a point to speak to people whose judgment I trust — this is especially helpful in revealing aspects of the situation I may have missed. By this time, I should have a good sense of what action I need to take. Once I am sure it is the right thing to do, I get on and do it quickly. Procrastination is no one's friend; and the longer I wait, the more likely I am to chicken out of potentially risky or courage-requiring actions.

It is possible that after reflection you come to the conclusion that you were backing up the wrong tree. Admitting that one has failed is never easy, and it takes courage to make the decision to put a full stop on something that is not working. One of the first businesses I started many years ago failed within its first 12 months. My friend and I had this wonderful idea about a clothing range for a specific target market. We were incredibly passionate about our concept and the customers we would be serving. We never for one moment thought that we wouldn't succeed — perhaps we were naïve. We did everything we could do right — or so we thought.

A few months into the business, I realised I was going to have to make the difficult decision to shut it all down; but, still, we limped along for a few more months, just because I didn't want to do what had to be done. Failing at just about anything can be very painful. Not only does it make us question our abilities, it also challenges us to the very core of our identity. Every time we fail at something, we have some choices to make. We can choose to let the failure crush us and bring us to the point where we never want to try again, or we can choose to learn what we can from it and move on. Fortunately, on this occasion, I chose the latter.

The secret to dealing with pressures that threaten to derail us from our planned journeys is to keep our 'why' at the forefront of our thinking as much as we can. Your 'why' is the reason you do what you do. It's the final destination you are headed for and the benefits getting to that destination will bring. There is usually a big 'why' — your ultimate purpose for existing — but there are also small 'whys' along the way. These small 'whys' are the steps necessary for you to live out the big 'why'. On the days that you feel like quitting, think about why you started in the first place. Think about what you'll lose if you give up before you achieve what you are aiming for. If your 'why' is big enough, you will have the motivation you need to keep trying; and if it's not, well, perhaps it's time to find a 'why' that *is* big enough. I like the lyrics to this song by Michael Smith. Read it slowly and allow the words to sink in, then pick yourself up and have another go.

This is what you're made for
Standing in the downpour
Knowing that the sun will shine
Forget what lies behind you
Heaven walks beside you
You got to give it one more try
One more time

The secret to dealing with pressures that threaten to derail us from our planned journeys is to keep our 'why' at the forefront of our thinking as much as we can.

Ask yourself:

1. What are the obstacles I am facing right now that I need to deal with?
2. What steps can I take to overcome them?
3. How can I be better prepared in the future for similar challenges that might arise?
4. Whose wise counsel do I need to seek right now?

Step Eight

Embracing the Mundane

In between goals is a thing called life; that has to be lived and enjoyed – **Sid Caesar**

I would love to say that once you have figured out what your purpose is and have started to take steps in the direction of fulfilling that purpose, that your life will be one great exciting adventure. But I would be lying to you, and that's the last thing I want to do. Yes, there are days when you'll feel like you are powering ahead at full speed like a super charged race car; but equally, there will be days when you think even a snail could make more progress; or worse still, days when it feels like you have taken a few steps backwards. So, the question isn't, 'will there be days like this?' but instead 'what do I do with this sort of days?'

Often, when I initially start to work with a client, they may seem to be making great progress in a very short time compared to what they were able to achieve before we started to work together; as such, they are not always prepared to face the slow periods that are inevitable. One of my practices is to get my clients to complete a coach preparation form before every session. This is as much for their benefit as it is for mine. Pam is a very accomplished businesswoman who was looking to increase her productivity in one of her businesses. She came to one of our sessions, despondent, because she felt she had not accomplished as much as she had hoped since the last time we met.

As I read out from her coach preparation form what she had achieved, she was astounded by the fact that she had done so much in just four weeks. This is not an uncommon occurrence, especially in high achievers. They tend to just power on without stopping to look back at the result of what they have accomplished and this can result in them feeling as though they are not doing enough. Does this resonate with you?

The first thing to do on days when it seems like you are not making adequate progress is to stop and assess what you have achieved so far — you might be pleasantly surprised. Even if you do discover that you really haven't achieved as much as you would have hoped, berating yourself is likely to make you feel worse than you already do. Who needs that? Rather than spending precious time ruminating over what could have been, it would be more productive for you to determine where you might have gone off track and come up with a plan that will get you back on track.

Secondly, you might need a paradigm shift in your thinking. Contrary to the picture often painted by motivational speakers (and I have been guilty of this myself in the past), life is not meant to be lived at full speed *all the time.* Imagine what it would feel like to ride a roller coaster that never comes to an end. I am not a fan of roller coasters at the best of times, so the thought of being on one for longer than is absolutely necessary is disheartening. Even for those people that thrive on the thrill of a ride on Death Wish, or some similarly labelled roller coaster, getting back to the ground in one piece is always a relief.

In response to the excitement (or fright, as the case may be) of a ride like that, the body releases chemicals that are responsible for the physical effects — like an increase in your heart rate, sweating, increased focus, surge of energy, and that stomach-flipping feeling we are all familiar with. Noradrenaline, adrenaline, and cortisol are the hormones responsible for these responses that occur when you are faced with what the brain perceives as a threat. There are other hormones that affect the body's response to stress, but these are the main three.

While the effects of the hormones mentioned above can save your life in a dangerous situation — by causing you to fight or flee — sustained amounts in the blood stream is bad news. They are called stress hormones because they have the potential to cause high blood pressure, stomach ulcers, and other illnesses. In addition, too much cortisol can suppress the immune system, increase blood sugar, decrease libido, produce acne, and contribute to obesity. After a stressful event, it can take hours or even days for the body to return to its original state. Even stewing over problems, or worrying, can lead to continued release of cortisol, and therefore, increased stress.

Using the analogy of the roller coaster ride as a backdrop, you can see how sustained periods of intense activity can have negative consequences. My firm belief is that the mundane aspects of our lives constitute gifts that help us avoid burnout. This may sound rich coming from someone who would race through life from one thing to the next rather than stand still, and if you are anything like me, you would understand too well the frustration of standing still when you could be running. Still, the truth is that mundane is good for us.

The most exciting thing in your day right now may be paying the electricity bill — celebrate that. Your mind needs the respite that everyday run of the mill activities afford you. These activities stop you from going into overdrive. There is something strangely calming about repetitive actions that require minimal involvement of the higher executive functions of the brain. Like the calm after a storm, ordinary days help you recover whilst at the same time preparing you for your next big push. Rather like the ebb and flow of the tide, there is a healthy rhythm of living that will make your life's journey less hazardous.

One of the most effective ways to deal with the humdrum of life while still being intentional about living out your purpose starts with an attitude change. Based on the information you now have about the importance of downtime, you can choose to celebrate each day, regardless of what it brings. Instead of moaning about the ordinariness of life in between important accomplishments, you can find ways of refreshing your mind and body. Building enjoyable activities into your daily or weekly schedule will ensure that when there is a lull in focused activity, you are not left twiddling your thumbs. Doing something you enjoy helps you relax and re-energize, preparing you for the next thing.

I often encourage my clients to build rewards into their journey as they pursue their goals. For each milestone they reach on the Stepping Stones model I mentioned earlier, I encourage them to decide how they will reward themselves. Rewards don't have to be lavish or expensive, they just have to be activities or things that are refreshing or bring you joy. Spending a day out with a loved one, or treating yourself to a personal item or activity that you will enjoy, does not have to cost the earth. One client I coached could not remember the last time she bought herself an item of clothing. She was so focused on making her business successful whilst looking after her four children that shopping was not on her agenda. Somehow, she felt she didn't deserve to spend any money on herself until she had made enough of it. It was no surprise that when I asked her to choose a reward to look forward to after she achieved her first goal, her choice was shopping!

It is time to ditch the erroneous idea that busyness always equates to productivity — it doesn't. Or the belief that people won't respect you if you admit to not being particularly busy during some periods of your life. Being busy is not a badge of honour that we wear in an attempt to impress people. If your life is fruitful and productive, that's what people will see, not the fact that you always appear to be chasing your tail. Make the most of quiet days - use them for relaxation or as times of reflection and planning your next step.

Great ideas surface during times of reflection or apparent inactivity; therefore, expect solutions to problems and fresh ideas on ways you can use your skills and talents more profitably. I have had many a brilliant idea whilst ironing or washing up — chores I don't particularly like. It is at times like these that I am really grateful for the mundane. There will be many ordinary days and fewer extraordinary ones in your lifetime. So, learn to celebrate each season of your life — life will be much more fulfilling and much less frustrating if you do.

It is time to ditch the erroneous idea that busyness always equates to productivity.

Ask yourself

1. What is my attitude towards aspects of my life that I find ordinary?
2. How good am I at making time for relaxation and reflection?
3. What needs to change so that when I find myself in a quiet period I would still have things I can do to refresh and re-energize myself?

Part Three
The Flow

We keep moving forward, opening new doors, and doing new things, because we're curious and curiosity keeps leading us down new paths – **Walt Disney**

One

Staying Motivated

If you have a strong purpose in life, you don't have to be pushed. Your passion will drive you there – **Roy T. Bennett**

What a great feeling! You have figured out what you were made for. You've cut out the clutter that was distracting you, and you are now focusing on your purpose with laser-like precision. You've taken your first steps towards this new fulfilling life, and you are having the time of your life while doing it. Who thought that using your skills and talents to serve others could be so rewarding? Even the mundane tasks that previously had you frustrated now serve as a necessary pause to help you recharge and refuel. Life has not felt so good in a long time.

Amidst all this, there is a small part of you that is apprehensive because you don't think this state of euphoria will last. Someday, in the near future, you might be thinking, it will all fall apart and you will be back where you started, wondering what your life is all about. You are concerned you'll be left worse off than you were before you discovered that living on purpose could be so exciting.

It doesn't have to be like that. You can stay motivated and continue to live your life with intentionality and focus. I am not saying there won't be days when you feel about as excited as a child visiting the dentist for the first time. Challenges and bad hair days are inevitable, but they don't have to distract you from the life you've set out to live. They don't have the power to cause you to draw the conclusion that living a life of purpose is not worth pursuing; unless you let them.

The trick to staying motivated is to give yourself a reason to stay motivated. No big revelation, right? But it's the simple things we know but don't do that have the potential to keep us stuck. Learning how to motivate yourself will mean you don't have to wait until you can listen to a motivational talk or read a book in order to maintain your enthusiasm for life. For example, if providing a bright future for my children by working hard for financial increase is important enough to me, then I will drag myself through my worst days to achieve that purpose. But if it isn't, well, I will probably give up at the first difficulty or challenge; or, perhaps the second; most definitely the third.

Your life purpose has to be big enough to withstand the storms of life. That is partly why it can't just be about you. If it was just about you, chances are, you won't want to go the long haul. When other people or causes you care about stand to benefit from your actions, you are more likely to stay motivated; unless you're a really selfish person. But I don't think you are; otherwise, you wouldn't be reading this book in the first place.

I refer to this concept as identifying your Big Why. Your Big Why is the reason you want to live your life on purpose and achieve certain dreams and goals. Sometimes, as mentioned earlier, it could be because of what it would mean for your nearest and dearest. At other times, an experience you had in the past — negative or positive — can result in you deciding that you would like to live a certain way and contribute to society in a meaningful way. Whatever your Big Why is, it has to be big enough to affect you in a way that keeps you going in spite of the challenges you will face as you pursue your goals and dreams.

Leaving my medical practice for a future that was anything but clear was a tough decision to make. I had no guarantee of success and did not even have a solid plan for what I was going to do next. I knew, however, without a shadow of doubt, that I owed it to myself to explore the possibilities. During my 'year out' I rediscovered a passion inside me that had been buried for a long time — helping people achieve their dreams and fulfil their potential. The fact that I could work flexibly and therefore have more time with my family was a much-welcomed added bonus.

The first few years were tough. There were days when I questioned the wisdom of my decisions. In the long run, what kept me going was the satisfaction I got from seeing people that I had the privilege of working with astound themselves and others by what they achieved. Every time I took an impromptu day off to enjoy a girly day out with my daughter, or have coffee with my son after picking him up from school, I was reminded of the reason why I had taken a leap in the dark by setting up a Coaching Practice. This was part of living the new life I was determined to live.

It is possible that a counter argument would be that I was helping sick people when I was a Medical Doctor. Surely, that should have been fulfilling enough? Perhaps, but my work as a doctor was not making full use of *all* my gifts and talents — which included teaching, public speaking, and developing people. Now I feel like I have the best of both worlds. I not only have the privilege of helping sick people get better a few days a month, I get to do all the other things I truly love doing — like running training workshops, coaching, and writing. My Big Why keeps me going even when I am having the worst day imaginable.

Some examples of Big Whys that past clients have had include: 'having enough to provide for my aging parents', 'building a business that employees love to work in and one that will make me proud' and 'changing people's perception of mental health'.

Once you have identified your Big Why, the next step is to make sure this reason stays in the forefront of your thinking. There are many ways of achieving this, and what you choose will depend in part on what holds your attention the most. As someone who loves words, it is no surprise that I keep a journal where I write down thoughts, ideas, goals, and prayers. I also put down the steps I intend to take towards achieving my goals, and I revisit my journal regularly. It's my way of reminding myself about the things that are important to me, so I can keep track of my actions and make sure these actions are in keeping with my aspirations.

If you tend to prefer visual prompts, you can put some pictures in a prominent place like on the refrigerator or your workstation. Vision boards are quite popular in coaching circles. This is a board where you display images of where you want to go or what you want to be; it is a tool that helps you clarify and maintain focus on your goals. In these days of information overload and a million and one distractions, a vision board can act as a constant prompt to stay focused. Vision boards are easy to make and can even be made on your computer or tablet. I once had as my screen saver, a picture reminding me of a goal I had. This meant I couldn't get away from it — every time I turned on my tablet, there it was!

Your Big Why can change during different phases of your life — there is nothing wrong with that. Hopefully, as we grow and develop, we also change and our priorities change depending on what is going on inside us. If you discover that your Big Why no longer motivates you as it used to, it could mean it's time to have a rethink. Your Big Why must be compelling, relevant, and worthwhile.

Another effective way to stay motivated is to take a long view of your journey. Things have a way of taking longer than expected, and it is easy to get discouraged when the journey seems to be slower than you envisaged at the beginning. Instead of allowing frustration rob you of the joy of living, it is wise to adopt the thinking that the length of time it takes to get to your destination is not nearly as important as getting there. Sometimes, you will make quick progress; but at other times, things will be slower than you prefer. That's life; don't let that get to you. Success that is worth having often comes slowly.

In his book, *Never Too Late To Be Great: The Power Of Thinking Long*, Tom Butler-Bowdon says:

It is the nature of true success that at first, even for a long time, it seems like nothing is happening. In despair, we think that we have picked the wrong ingredients or got the recipe wrong. Peering into the oven, we see nothing. But come back later, and suddenly we discern a dark mass rising above the rim of the tin. Things of value often come into being too slowly for us to notice, working on timescales beyond normal apprehension. Just as the human eye cannot 'see' plants growing in real time, but only notice growth in hindsight, so we often cannot appreciate the progress we have made.

I remind myself of this truth when life is less than exciting and the results I am getting appear to have a negative relationship to the effort I am putting in. It is a truth that is all too easy to forget in the madness of chasing after goals and juggling work and relationships at the same time. It is a truth that will cause us to take a deep breath and slow down; trusting that we are doing our part and the rest is not up to us. Too often, we look at people who have 'succeeded' in our eyes, but we fail to see that their success has been preceded by months, and sometimes years, of gruelling hard work that no one but them knows about. We can get sucked into a culture that expects instant results and gain without commensurate pain.

Seth Godin, author and entrepreneur says:

We need to stop looking for lightning bolts. You don't win an Olympic medal with a few weeks of intensive training. There's no such thing as an overnight opera sensation. Every great thing has been built in exactly the same way: bit by bit, step by step, little by little. There are no short cuts; you must be willing to pay the price.

The trick to staying motivated is to give yourself a reason to stay motivated.

Ask yourself:

1. How motivated am I with my life purpose at the moment?
2. What is my Big Why and how can I make sure I keep it in the fore front of my thinking as much as I can?
3. What truths can I focus on when I don't feel very motivated?
4. Where, perhaps, do I need to give myself a break, take a deep breath and take a longer view of what I am trying to achieve?

Two

Falling and Failing

*Failures are finger posts on the road to achievement – **C.S Lewis***

I said earlier that one of my first businesses failed within its first year. I can admit it easily now without a great degree of emotion or regret but it was a while before I could do this. Failing at just about anything can be very painful. There is something about the prospect of failing or falling that causes fear in most people. This fear stops people from taking risks, which by the nature of what they represent, always carry the possibility of failure. This fear also makes us question our abilities, and challenges us to the very core of who we believe we are.

For many, failing seems to be the proof that they are not good enough, smart enough, committed enough, and the list goes on and on. While any of the aforementioned reasons for failure might be valid, your mistakes do not define you. The only circumstance in which your mistakes define you is when you keep making the same ones over and over again instead of learning from them and getting it right the next time you face a similar scenario. Every time you fail at something, you have some choices to make. You can choose to let the failure crush you and bring you to the point where you never want to try again or you can choose to learn what you can and move on — it's called getting back on your horse.

Since my above-mentioned business wound up, I have failed at many other things and probably will fail at many more in the future. On the flip side, I have also succeeded a great deal at more — that is the nature of truly living. You can't wait until you are sure you will succeed before you even try. That is not what people who end up succeeding do. One of the early developmental milestones that babies achieve is learning to walk. When was the last time you saw a toddler in the process of learning to walk, sit down in the dirt after he or she had fallen for perhaps the hundredth time and refuse to try again? Or decide to sit on the floor for the rest of their lives? No, of course they don't do that; they pick themselves up and try again. And each time they choose to try again, they become even more determined to walk. Unless they have a health issue, most toddlers eventually grasp the skill of walking.

One of the most quoted failures is that of Thomas Edison, an American investor and business man who discovered the electric light bulb. He is quoted as saying: "I have not failed. I've just found 10,000 ways that won't work." Many of us have heard this quote but gloss over it without putting ourselves in his shoes and feeling what he might have felt as he carried out the ninety-ninth experiment or the five-hundredth — or even the one before he achieved what he had been aiming for. He refused to give up because he saw failure not as a red 'stop' sign, but as an amber 'get ready to go' sign.

Failure is never final — at least, not until you decide to give up and quit trying. Some of the lessons I learned from my failed business are still keeping me in good stead years after the event. If you allow it, failure can teach you more lessons than success ever could. The lessons you learn when you fail at something are marked more indelibly in your memory than the ones you learn after you become successful. There is something about persevering through failure that builds character in a way that success never can. Don't get me wrong, I am just as passionate about succeeding as the next person, but I have come to realise that success hardly ever happens without failure; and the more I fail, the more likely I am to succeed. The fact that I am failing shows that I am trying. The only guarantee that you won't fail is if you never even try. Unfortunately, never trying is also the only guarantee that you will never succeed.

Have you failed at something recently? Do you find yourself having to admit that something you believed in hasn't worked out like you hoped it would? You are not alone. One of the clients I worked with a number of years ago was having some difficulty making a career progression. While Tracy had the qualifications to apply for a senior management job in the education field, she was hesitant to do this. As she talked during one of our coaching sessions, it became clear that one of the reasons she couldn't seem to make up her mind about what job to apply for was because she had made decisions in the past that in retrospect, seemed to have been the wrong ones. Subsequently, she no longer trusted her ability to make the right decision, and this affected not just her work life but her personal life as well.

Tracy wanted some assurance that she would never make the wrong decision again. I couldn't give her that assurance — no one could. So instead of seeking false assurances, we focused on how she had handled failure in the past. We explored how she could change her view of failing so that in future she would not be paralysed by the decisions she had made in the past that hadn't resulted in good outcomes. We also spent some time looking at her decision-making process to make sure it was based on sound principles. But the bottom line was she needed to learn to give herself permission to fail. She needed to develop a system for handling her failure and learning from it.

By the time we had concluded our sessions, she had applied for and got a job in a senior management position. And because changes in one area of your life often spill over into other areas, she had also started taking more risks in her personal relationships. Her view of failing had changed; all she needed was an attitude change.

This quote by Eloise Ristad says: *"When we give ourselves permission to fail, we, at the same time give ourselves permission to excel."* What a profound statement!

Many people have regrets at the end of their lives — things they did which they wish they hadn't. And while this may be very painful, there is another kind of regret that haunts people as they take their last breath — the chances they never took. Those 'what ifs' that you'll never know the answer to, because it's too late to go back and find out what would have happened if you had left that job sooner, taken that risk with your business, enrolled in that course, taken that person on as a partner .... the list is endless.

It is tragic but true that many people will live and die without ever achieving the things they really wanted to; or lived the life they had dreamed they could; built the business or team they believed they were capable of; found the financial freedom they hoped they would. I could go on and on listing lost dreams and failed hopes; but I won't. Instead, I want to ask the question, why? Why do so many people fail to achieve what they had the potential to achieve?

There are many reasons for this, but by far the most common is the fear of failure. Fear of failure will lead to missed opportunities and unfulfilled dreams. This fear of failure is often closely linked to a fear of criticism and rejection. We don't attempt things we think we might fail at because we are worried about how others will see us. We procrastinate because we believe it is better if we did not try at all than to have to nurse the pain of disappointment that invariably accompanies failure. We hesitate to make changes because we are not assured of what lies on the other side of change.

In his book: *"Who Moved My Cheese?"* the author, Ken Blanchard, tells the story of a mouse that is so afraid of the unknown that he is unwilling to do anything about his circumstances even though his current means of survival is threatened. Fear is a very powerful emotion and it has the ability to literally paralyze us. Have you ever stood in front of a crowd and felt so nervous that your salivary glands ceased to function and your lips just would not move?

Successful people have learned to overcome their fears in order to move forward. They have learned to "feel the fear and do it anyway", as so aptly put by Susan Jeffers. One of the questions that stood out for me in Ken Blanchard's book mentioned earlier was, "what would you do if you weren't afraid?" It led me down a path of reflecting on how my fears were stopping me in my tracks and I had to decide what I was going to do in order to deal with these fears.

Is it possible to overcome this fear of failure? Absolutely. Successful people have learned to see failure as feedback rather than evidence of their capabilities (or lack of it); as a pothole that is surmountable rather than a roadblock that is impassable. Feedback provides information that can eventually lead to a successful outcome. Failure is not final. We learn from making mistakes, and from what doesn't work, allowing us to discover what does work. Trial and error becomes the means of finding solutions to life's challenges.

Fear of failure will affect how you view risk taking, and this will in turn affect your confidence. While unnecessary risk taking is not a recommended way of approaching life, some degree of risk is needed to develop your talents or skills, explore new opportunities, or change an aspect of your life that is not working. A healthy way of looking at failure is to see it as an opportunity to learn rather than evidence that something is wrong with you. Rather than taking the failure too personally, thereby reducing your chances of turning things around, you look objectively at what went wrong and how you might have created a different outcome.

Your attitude to failure is dependent on your personality as well as the kind of environment you grew up in. If you were not given the room to make mistakes, then you will most probably try as much as possible to avoid making one. The same goes for work environments where employees are expected to get it right all the time — what a creativity killer this kind of environment can be. When you think you will be penalized heavily for making a mistake, you are less likely to try anything that does not have a guarantee of success.

As you start to live purposefully, you will make mistakes. You will take paths that will feel right at first only for you to discover somewhere along the way that you missed it; and that's ok. There is some degree of trial and error with working out what you are supposed to be doing with the rest of your life. If it were so easy, many more people would be living purposeful and fulfilling lives. Staying focused is hard work. Establishing boundaries that help you refuse to get involved in activities that waste your time, and ultimately your life, requires constant recalibration of what is important and what isn't. You need to decide from the outset that no matter how many times you get it wrong, you won't quit.

The first step in dealing with failure is to acknowledge what has happened — you missed it; you made the wrong call; you missed the opportunity that was presented to you. Take responsibility for what you did and take a deep breath to remind yourself that it is not the end of the road. You may have hit a pothole or even a roadblock, but the delay is only temporary and there is a way around it. It is important not to make any snap decisions that you might later regret. I once read somewhere that if you have a big decision to make, then making sure you are not sad, tired, or angry goes a long way in ensuring you don't make the wrong decision. If you have just failed at something, or fallen, one or all of these emotions are likely to be prevalent.

Once you are feeling less emotional, take some time to reflect on what happened, making sure to separate the person (you) from whatever happened (the event). This will ensure your conclusions are not tainted by unnecessary emotion. Start with acknowledging what you did right — however insignificant it may have seemed at the time. Ask yourself what you could have done differently. This is where learning happens. Sometimes, it is helpful to do this with a close friend, colleague, partner, or coach. Be kind to yourself; but at the same time, don't make excuses.

After a failure, particularly a major one, it is easy to be so afraid of it happening again that you are reluctant to try anything new. You need to 'get back on your horse' as soon as possible. Don't let the fear of failure keep you paralysed from moving forward. The chances of success are more likely if you refuse to give up in spite of your failures.

While unnecessary risk taking is not a recommended way of approaching life, some degree of risk is needed to develop your talents or skills, explore new opportunities, or change an aspect of your life that is not working.

Ask yourself:
1. How do I view failure?
2. What past failures am I allowing to have a negative impact on my present decisions?
3. Where do I need to give myself permission to fail?
4. What calculated risks do I need to take as I go forward?

Three

Making Adjustments

Every success story is the tale of constant adaptation, revision and change – **Richard Branson**

During the first year of running my coaching business, I coached anyone that came within touching distance; well, almost anyone. Excited that I had discovered something I was truly passionate about, something that had the potential to transform lives, I was eager to help everyone I met achieve their goals and live the life they had only dreamed of. I coached my children, my husband and my friends during informal conversations, until they cottoned on to what I was doing and started resisting!

I didn't need to do much in the way of marketing in my first year. I was transitioning from full time medical practice, and clients who I got from word of mouth referrals took up what time I did have for coaching. However, this all changed in my second year when all of a sudden my bank of clients dried up. I found myself facing up to the fact that as much as I disliked the thought, I was going to have to do some intentional marketing if I was still going to have a business by the end of the year. It was at this point that I realized that in order to market effectively, I needed to identify my target market. This was extremely difficult for me, because I did not want to have to say no to any potential clients. I really did have an overwhelming desire to help everyone that came my way. But anyone that has run a successful business knows that you cannot be everything to everyone. So I had to choose.

The ultimate goal — to help people achieve their dreams and live intentional and fulfilled lives — had not changed. I just needed to decide which group or groups of people I was most passionate about serving. After a few weeks of thinking about this, I decided that based on the training I had received and the fact that I was really passionate about raising leaders in the corporate and not-for-profit sectors, rebranding as a Leadership and Business coach was my next logical step

This meant that I had to have my website re-designed to portray this new direction, have new business cards printed, and change my profile on all my social media accounts. It seemed like a lot of work but I knew it was the right thing to do, so I just rode the pain. As you take carefully planned steps to accomplish your life purpose, you'll have to remain flexible so that you can make adjustments as they become necessary. Often, the steps you are taking were planned with limited information about what the future would hold, what would be a good fit for you, or what results (or lack of it) your actions would yield. Rather like a sailor adjusts his or her sails in response to the wind, you would do well to prepare yourself for any changes you may have to make as you go along.

Note that the sailor does not change his destination unless he got that wrong in the first place; he merely changes the route he will take to get there. I often describe coaching to my clients as a process rather like peeling an onion — until you start to take off the layers you don't really see what's beneath. Taking off layers often involves action of some sort so as to reveal what is really at the heart of the individual. This process of peeling reveals what is really of value to them and what they are capable of doing. I love the *eureka* moment when my clients discover that what they thought was something they really wanted was merely a smoke screen for what they really wanted. This discovery would not have been made if they hadn't started walking towards what they thought they wanted. It is easier to steer a moving car than a stationary one. Remaining flexible about the approach you take to fulfilling your dreams and goals also means that you are better placed to handle disappointments and challenges that you may face along the way.

I mentioned a client I worked with sometime ago, Pam. At the time we started working together, she owned and ran three businesses. She had assumed one of them — one that had to do with multi-level marketing — was the one that needed her attention the most at the time because it was not doing as well as expected. As we started to look at the reason for the poor performance, it transpired that the business needing her focus at that point in time was her main business — the one she had invested most of her money and time in. But because of difficult relationships at work, she was choosing to sideline that business in order to focus on one where she had more control and less conflict. Once she realized this, she made the necessary adjustments, found ways to deal with her work environment, and developed better focus and productivity as a result.

Maintaining flexibility does not mean you lose focus or forget what the ultimate goal is; it simply means that you are prepared to try other ways of accomplishing your goal if circumstances beyond your control threaten to take you off track. It also means that you are prepared to make mistakes and learn from them. The discovery that perhaps your intended destination is not the right one after all and therefore needs altering is better made sooner rather than later. It is not the end of the road for you, as you can change course at any time. I like the way John Maxwell puts it in this quote:

Failed plans should not be interpreted as a failed vision. Visions don't change, they are only refined. Plans rarely stay the same, and are scrapped or adjusted as needed. Be stubborn about the vision but flexible with the plan.

There has to be a degree of proactivity about stopping every so often to take stock of what you have achieved so far and what's still ahead. Taking stock at regular intervals is good practice and helps you determine whether you are still on course or whether there are some adjustments that need to be made to your journey. It would not make much sense to set out with the aim of travelling north only to discover many miles later that you have arrived at a destination, only its north-west rather than the intended north.

Taking stock involves spending time to look back every few weeks or months, asking yourself a few pertinent questions. What were you aiming for when you started? Are your goals still valid or have they changed? Have you discovered, for example, that the job you thought would tick all the boxes of your ideal job suddenly doesn't seem quite so appealing because it doesn't fit in with your core values? Or perhaps the stakes for that life you envisioned are higher than you initially thought and therefore you need to reconsider your willingness to make the sacrifices required.

Providing your goals and dreams are still valid and worth pursuing, the next step is to look at where you are in relation to where you are headed. What progress have you made so far? What has worked well? What hasn't worked so well? Ditch what hasn't worked and try a different approach. Keep making adjustments until you hit the jackpot. Think outside the box, and be willing to seek counsel.

Finally, taking stock also involves looking ahead to your destination and making sure you have the resources you need to get there. Re-assess your skills and talents and the human resources you have at your disposal. Decide what else you might need, and take steps to ensure you can get everything you need. Don't be too hard on yourself if you are not as far along as you had hoped; things often take longer than expected, and if we don't guard against it, we can let the passage of time discourage us from pressing on. Remind yourself that Rome was not built in a day, and things of value often take a long time to build. Learn to be your own greatest cheerleader — it's not every time there'll be someone else to cheer you on in your dark moments of discouragement. Many times, you are the only one who can bring yourself out of the pit of despair.

Taking stock at regular intervals is good practice and helps you determine whether you are still on course or whether there are some adjustments that need to be made to your journey.

Ask yourself:
1. How often will I stop to take stock of my achievements so

far?
2. How determined am I to keep pressing on no matter what?
3. How flexible am I when things don't go as planned?
4. What attitude changes may need to take place in me to avoid the disappointment that can happen with delay in my progress?

Four

Your Best Self

> *There is nothing noble in being superior to your fellow man; true nobility is being superior to your former self.* — **Ernest Hemingway**

I once heard an executive coach make this statement: "at some point in our lives, we all need a mentor, a coach, and a counsellor." While I don't completely agree with this view, I can understand his reasoning. The only way to become your best self is to keep learning and developing. Often, this is not something that can be achieved in isolation. The bottom line is that we need help from others if we are to become the best version of ourselves. So many times, our friends and family love us too much to point out areas where we might be falling short. You may not feel like you are in need of all the three professionals mentioned above, but the journey you have undertaken is one that is more likely to succeed if you have the right person or persons cheering you on and helping you through some of the bumpy patches.

The Johari window is a tool that coaches often use with their clients. Devised by American psychologists, Joseph Luft and Harry Ingham, in 1955, while they were researching group dynamics at the University of California, Los Angeles, it helps increase self-awareness and relationships between individuals in a group. Several adaptations have since been made to the original model and it is being used in personal development, group work, and to improve communication. The basis of this model is that we all have blind spots, aspects of our personalities that we don't reveal to others, and equally as important, things we don't know that we don't know about ourselves. It is only as we start to have conversations with other people that some of these 'hidden' aspects of our personalities begin to unravel to enable us to work on them and hopefully become better people.

Personal development is about growing and developing so that we can become better people. Some of this growth happens without much thought (a bit like physical growth) just by living from one day to the next. However, a considerable amount of growth must be intentional if it is to happen at all. When my daughter was much younger, she got to a point where she felt like she had got to her maximum height in life and didn't want to grow any taller. It was really funny because I knew that she didn't have much of a say in whether or not she was going to grow taller, as genes and nutrition rather than her desire would determine her final height.

With personal growth or development, however, it's somewhat different. We often have to make the choice to grow; otherwise, we could remain the same person for years despite countless opportunities to grow. This personal choice is the reason why even though two people go through the same difficult circumstances, one can develop into a stronger, wiser, or more compassionate person while the other remains bitter and trapped in the past. It is why we sometimes describe some adults as immature. Their bodies have developed into adulthood but their personalities and thinking have not grown to the same degree.

The word 'grow' means 'to increase in size by a natural process'. It can also mean to expand or to gain. If you look at the kind of growth that happens with plants, for example, certain conditions have to be present for the plant to grow. Let's take a farmer who plants a kernel of corn as an example. This seed has an innate ability to become a corncob. If the farmer just plants the seed in the ground and folds his arms, there is no guarantee that the seed will germinate. Yes, there is a strong possibility that it might, given that rain and sunshine are natural phenomena that facilitate growth. But if this farmer wants the assurance of a good crop of corn, he will have to make sure his seeds are planted on fertile ground in the first place. He needs to ensure that the seeds are exposed to sufficient water and sunshine. Finally, he needs to keep the birds away from his seeds. And when harvest time comes, he needs to make sure the corn is harvested on time so that the fruit does not begin to dry out or rot.

There is more chance of success at living a life that is both purposeful and significant if you have an intention to improve yourself continually. You need to be able to look back at the years and clearly see your development as a person. This growth generally doesn't happen automatically (although this is not impossible, it is unlikely that growth will be sustained without your active participation). Growth on the outside (business, career, relationships, etc.) is more often than not preceded by growth that happens on the inside — the way you think, the way you perceive yourself and others, and the way you handle emotions. Often people get this order wrong; they try to grow something on the outside when they are not ready on the inside to handle that growth.

Invariably, personal development requires a disciplined approach. It takes time, money, and effort to improve yourself, and quite frankly, a lot of us would rather stick with the status quo than do something to change it. Change is tricky at the best of times, and many people do not navigate change very well, especially when that change has something to do with their thoughts and behaviours. How many times have you heard the phrase 'if it ain't broke, don't fix it'? Human beings are creatures of habit; there is comfort in the familiar, and the unknown tends to cause more anxiety than the here and now. Reading books, attending training courses, and hiring a coach or mentor are all ways that one can improve themselves. These things cost money and time, but can you afford not to do whatever you can to become your best self?

There is also some humility required in any personal development endeavour because you are admitting to yourself and to others that there are aspects of your personality, character, knowledge, or skills that need work. Only a big-headed person will think they have achieved everything, and therefore, is not in need of further work in the areas I previously mentioned. Humility is an attribute that is especially attractive in anyone who is in a leadership position as evidenced in the book *Good to Great* by Jim Collins. Even if you are not in a position of leadership, staying humble will mean that you remain teachable and open to change as you pursue your goals and dreams. This doesn't mean that you will accept every criticism and try to please everyone; you just have to be selective about the people you give permission to speak into your life.

One of the reasons I am so passionate about coaching is that it is a process by which the coachee's awareness is increased so that change can happen. The right kind of coach creates a safe and affirming environment where the coachee feels empowered to make the right choices for themselves even if these choices involve changing some aspects of their thoughts or behaviours. This is because they know the change will bring them closer to their goals. A mentor can achieve the same objective, but very often, the mentor presents their own experience of their journey, and this may not always be a good fit for the mentee. In some cases, you may need both a mentor and a coach at different seasons in your journey. At some point, a counsellor may be required to help you deal with some events in your past that you want to make sense of. There is no hard and fast rule. The important thing is that you have the right help at the right time.

Personal development can also happen as part of a group. Surrounding yourself with people who are inspiring and optimistic can cause their attitude to rub off on you. If you have ever wondered why large successful companies have a board of directors, this is one of the reasons why. The company is more likely to succeed by bringing together a group of people who have a common goal or vision, as their combined wisdom, experience, and energy will lead to new ideas, and ultimately, growth. The concept of mastermind groups was first introduced by Napoleon Hill, the author of the famous book, Think and Grow Rich. He said this about these groups:

"No two minds ever come together without thereby creating a third, invisible intangible force, which may be likened to a third mind."

"The beauty of Mastermind Groups is that participants raise the bar by challenging each other to create and implement goals, brainstorm ideas, and support each other with total honesty, respect and compassion," says Karyn Greenstreet, owner of *Passion for Business* and a well-known Entrepreneur and Business Coach. Growing in a group can be just as effective (if not more) than growing on your own and it can be a bit more fun, like going to the gym with a friend or participating in a park run.

A few years ago, I was a bit stuck in the direction my business was going. I knew I needed a place where I could bounce ideas off other business owners and solopreneurs like myself, so I looked for a mastermind group to join. It was like looking for a needle in a haystack! I couldn't seem to find one that was close enough for me to get to. Finally, I came across a Business Coach that had a group about an hour and a half away from where I lived. Though it was far, it was by far the closest, and knowing that I needed this, I decided to join.

Over the next six months, we met once a month for about three hours each time. It was invaluable. Not only did I gain clarity about where I should be heading with my business, I was also able to diversify the services I was offering, with better results. I also gained the confidence to increase my fees because they helped me to see the value in the services I was offering. In addition, I had the satisfaction of helping the other members of the group with their own challenges and seeing their businesses grow and develop as a result. It really was a win-win. I was impacted by the experience enough to start my first mastermind group shortly afterwards, with good success.

Growth on the outside (business, career, relationships, etc.) is more often than not preceded by growth that happens on the

inside – the way you think, the way you perceive yourself and others, and the way you handle emotions.

Ask yourself:

1. How have I approached personal development in the past? With intention or haphazardly?
2. What plan do I have to develop myself over the next year, five years, or ten years?
3. How much am I willing to spend on developing myself in terms of time, money, and effort?
4. Identify two or three areas in your work or personal life that would be a good place to start.

Five

Enjoy the Ride

*Let your joy be in your journey - not in some distant goal - **Tim Cook***

As a coach, I help people make the transition from their current position to where they would like to be. This is a very goal-oriented pursuit; therefore, results and outcomes are very important. It's the same with discovering your life purpose and taking care to live that purpose out as best as you can. But we always need to keep things in perspective. I recently spent a weekend with some very dear friends. Although we engaged in deep conversations about life, we also had a lot of fun. Our conversations were spiced with lots of laughter. This time together with my friends made me realise that we don't take time off our careers to have fun as often as we should. Too often, in our pursuit of careers, goals or dreams, we forget to enjoy today on our way to tomorrow. The result is that while we may achieve what we set out to achieve, we get no real enjoyment of the process that got us there.

I have come to the conclusion that the journey is just as important (one could argue even more important) as the destination. While it is imperative that we constantly keep our eyes on the prize ahead (this will keep you motivated and focused), this should never be at the expense of enjoying every stage of our journey to the Promised Land. And I mean *every* stage. Even when there are challenges, we can still have aspects of our lives that we can be grateful for; enjoyable activities that we can engage in to minimise the effects of the difficulties. An important part of enjoying the journey involves learning as much as you can while traveling the road to your destination. It would be so easy to focus so hard on the destination that you miss out on precious moments in your life. Waiting until you reach your destination before you begin to enjoy your life is just not a fulfilling way to live. Work hard, but learn to play hard as well.

The pursuit of your goals will demand perseverance, hard work, focus, determination, and time. This can sometimes lead to emotional and physical fatigue, lack of motivation, and disappointment. There is always the temptation to give up before you reach your destination. Making sure that you take every opportunity to enjoy the journey will keep you enthusiastic, focused, and with recharged batteries when they are running low. I know I have started to slip on this very aspect of enjoying life when I find myself lacking in motivation. When this happens, I know it's time to stop and savour some precious moments of my present rather than be overly concerned about my future. Life is not meant to be one big slug. It is meant to be lived to the full. Every single day.

Some tips that will help you enjoy today on your way to tomorrow are:

> Don't take yourself too seriously. Learn to laugh often, and this includes laughing at yourself.
> Reward yourself for effort, not just results. You can't always predict that a certain action will bring great results, but at least you gave it a go. Your reward doesn't have to cost the earth — it could be a pamper day, a small gift to yourself, a favourite meal, etc.
> See setbacks as an opportunity to learn and grow. Don't be discouraged by them. Believe that you have what it takes to overcome them.
> Take up a hobby or develop an existing one. Make time in your diary regularly for this and don't feel guilty about spending this time doing something you love. You need it in order to keep yourself refreshed.
> Recognise special moments in your day and savour them. For example, a chance meeting with an old friend, a child wanting a cuddle, unplanned space in

your diary because a client has cancelled, etc. Don't be in such a hurry that you miss life's blessings, no matter how small.
➢ Maintain an attitude of gratitude. A thankful heart leads to a happy person.

Remember, today matters!!

Ask yourself:

1. Am I enjoying the journey as much as I could?
2. If not why not?
3. What am I going to do differently?

Six

Pass it On

Always remember people who have helped you along the way, and don't forget to lift someone up. — *Roy T. Bennett*

I love the word 'legacy' — it is rich with hope and promise. The thought that whatever I achieve in my life on earth could affect hundreds that come after I am gone is both humbling and challenging at the same time. The success of the next generation is dependent in part on the achievements of the generation who have lived before them, and on whose shoulders they stand. This thought is a game-changer that somehow has to affect the way we live our lives.

The word 'legacy' carries more connotation and weight than it seems at first glance. Most dictionaries define the word in financial terms — 'an amount of money or property left to someone in a will', but Dictionary.com goes on to add that it could be 'anything handed down from the past, as from an ancestor or predecessor'. Now, that puts a whole new spin on the word.

It's sad but true that many people don't think long-term. We get so caught up in the here and now that our decisions are made based on the present, and the furthest we can look ahead to is a few years. In his book, the Circle Maker, Mark Batterson tells the story of a letter the Swedish Navy received in 1980 telling them they had a shipment of lumber awaiting their collection. No one could remember having placed an order for lumber.

After some research, it turned out that the Swedish Parliament, recognising that it takes 150 years for an oak tree to mature, had ordered the planting of 20,000 oak trees on a Swedish island in 1929 because it anticipated there would be a shortage of lumber by the twenty first century. Years later, those fortunate Swedes were reaping the benefit of something they had no part in making — that's looking ahead. Most of those parliament members would have known they would not be alive by the time the wood was needed, but that knowledge did not stop them.

Whether we like it or not, our actions have just as much, if not more, impact on people around us than our words do. When we consider the effect our actions (or lack of it) could have on the next generation and the generation after, instead of just how it affects us, it will make us more intentional about what we do. Granted, there will be hard choices to make and there won't be any guarantees that we'll stick around long enough to see the fruit of our labour; but surely, that's no excuse not to do it anyway?

When you invest your money in a business venture, there is no guarantee of a good return; you may lose all that you have invested. Someone else may reap where you have sowed so tirelessly. When you invest your life in a cause, or in people, there are no guarantees either. There may be hurt, burnout, pain, and abandonment anywhere along the journey. As you have seen from reading this book, living a life of purpose will have its challenges and obstacles; but passing it on is a concept that is generous and fulfilling, and a recognition of the fact that some of the blessings we reap today are possible because of the sacrifices others made in the past.

I watched the movie *Suffragettes* a few weeks ago. It gave me an appreciation for the women (and men) who fought for the cause that allowed women to vote in the United Kingdom. Learning about the people who were involved in this struggle for equality forever changed my attitude towards the privilege I now have as a result. Lives and lifestyles were lost in that fight so that I don't have to fight the same battle ever again. True, there will be other battles to fight; but, hopefully, we build on the success of the courageous men and women that have gone before us, and the result is that the next generation doesn't have to fight the same battles we fought.

Remember the exercise you did in step two where you thought about what you would like to be read at your eulogy? This is where thinking long and hard is important. What would you like to leave behind for your children, colleagues, protégées, and friends? What would you like to be remembered by? If you didn't put any answers down when you did that exercise, now is the time to revisit that step.

The choices that you make when you take into consideration the effect it will have after you are gone will be different from those that you make without thinking long. When your thoughts are not just about how you will benefit from the choices you make and the actions you take, your life will truly take on a meaningfulness that might otherwise have been missing. When you fight for a cause that lives on after you have passed on, you fight harder and with more focus; you are also less likely to give up without a fight.

I make a point of always having someone I am mentoring. This involves me spending time with someone who doesn't pay me a dime, but in whom I have seen potential that needs developing. My aim is to impart as much as I can into them so they don't have to make the same mistakes or wrong choices that I made; this is my gift to the next generation. I see it as an investment that will benefit someone else in the future whether I am present in that future or not. I see everything I have learned in life as a benefit, not just for me, but for others as well.

Mentoring the younger generation is not the only way of leaving behind a legacy. Giving to worthy causes (whether that be time or money), writing, or using your voice to establish a better society for those coming after you are all ways of passing it on. Inventing processes or products that make life easier for a group or groups of people is another way of leaving a legacy. While I was writing this book, I was reminded of how fortunate I am that I haven't had to use a typewriter. Having to re-type a whole page because of one spelling error would have meant that a book of this size would have taken many more months to write than it has.

I am grateful to the person who invented the dishwasher, the washing machine, and the vacuum cleaner — keeping my house clean would have been a much more tedious job than it currently is. I am grateful for the lessons my parents taught me, which have helped me become the person I am today. The list is endless. One of the ways I show my gratitude for what I have received is to pass it on. It may take some thought for you to decide how, what, and to whom you can pass aspects of your life to; but it is certainly worth taking the time so that you are clear about the legacy that you will leave when you pass on from this world.

In the first part of this book, I mentioned the six human needs described by Anthony Robbins. The need for contribution is one of those six needs. To recap, it is the need to add value to the lives of others and to be part of something that is bigger than you; something that outlives you. Most people in areas of the world where basic needs like food, shelter, and security are met adequately, have this need. If you are reading this book, it is safe to assume that you do, too. This means that in order for your life to feel complete, you will need to think about the legacy you want to leave.

When you fight for a cause that lives on after you have passed on, you fight harder and with more focus; you are also less likely to give up without a fight.

Ask yourself:

1. What skills or life experiences do I have that will benefit someone else?
2. Who can I transfer these to?
3. What type of legacy would I like to leave behind?
4. How can I live my life with legacy in mind?

Conclusion

My aim in writing this book was first and foremost to provide proven steps for people who are yearning to live a life of purpose. I also wanted it be an authentic narrative of the highs and lows this pursuit might involve using examples from my own life and real life clients I have had the privilege to work with. It has been necessary to change the names of the people mentioned so as to protect their identities and to also respect their privacy. Although, writing this has been hard work, I have enjoyed every minute of it. I hope you have enjoyed reading it.

My prayer is that it will challenge and encourage you to start living your best life now. That kind of life is only possible when lived on purpose and with focused intentionality; but it is possible to live the life I have described in the pages of this book. It has been my honour to serve you. I would value your feedback. Please drop me a line about any aspect of the contents of the book.

Wishing you every success,

Oge Austin-Chukwu

Founder & Director

Reach Coaching

www.reach-coaching.com

info@reach-coaching.com

Notes

Batterson, Mark. *The Circle Maker: Praying Circles Around Your Biggest Dreams and Greatest Fears.* Reprint edition, Zondervan 2012

Buckingham, Marcus. *Find Your Strongest Life: What The Happiest and Most Successful Women do Differently.* International edition: Thomas Nelson 2009

Butler-Bowden, Tom. *Never Too Late To Be Great: The Power Of Thinking Long.* London, UK: Ebury Publishing, 2014

Covey, Steven R. *The Seven Habits of Highly Effective people: Powerful lessons in Personal Change.* London, UK. Simon & Schuster, 2004

Matthews, Gail. *Study Demonstrates That Writing Goals Enhances Goal Achievement.* Unpublished paper.

McMains, Stephanie and Sabine Kastner. *Interactions of Top-Down and Bottom-Up Mechanisms in Human Visual Cortex*, Journal of Neuroscience 12 January 2011, 31 (2) pg. 587-597

Resources

Secrets to Increased Confidence – a simple quick guide to becoming a confident woman.

This online course will help you increase your confidence in simple steps leading to noticeable change in just a few days. Designed as a course you can complete at your own pace and in the comfort of your own home, the material is downloadable and can be referred to again and again. Use the link below.

goo.gl/duCiqp

Stepping Stones Model - use link goo.gl/HSP85A

Mission Statement – use link goo.gl/7dL6dG

For other resources visit http://www.reach-coaching.com/resources/